UNIVERSITY OF CALIFORNIA, LOS ANGELES

BERKELEY · DAVIS · IRVINE · LOS ANGELES · MERCED · RIVERSIDE · SAN DIEGO · SAN FRANCISCO

UCLA

SANTA BARBARA · SANTA CRUZ

OFFICE OF THE CHANCELLOR
2147 MURPHY HALL, BOX 951405
LOS ANGELES, CALIFORNIA 90095-1405

Dear New Bruin,

You are about to embark upon one of the most exciting chapters in your life as a member of the incoming first year class. As a UCLA student, you will have access to the very best of what a university can be—a diverse community of talented people who enrich our society every day through hard work, intellectual exploration and active participation in the community.

UCLA's 2016–17 Common Book, Ta-Nehisi Coates' *Between the World and Me*, is an early part of this great adventure.

Our Common Book program serves as a springboard to building community on our campus and encouraging Bruins to contribute to the larger community beyond UCLA. *Between the World and Me* was chosen by a committee representing UCLA First Year Experience, UCLA Residential Life and other campus partners, as well as students and faculty. It will give us all an opportunity to share and understand diverse perspectives in a respectful way, explore our roles in creating a just society and consider steps we can take in response to the lessons shared by this compelling story.

Written in the form of a letter from a father to his son, *Between the World and Me* is both a personal portrayal of what it means to be black in America and a powerful critique of racism and segregation throughout our country's history. It offers a platform for us to engage in conversations around topics including race, American culture and history, the criminal justice system, the love that binds families and even the concept of college as a setting that inspires dialogue.

The discussions that will be prompted by our Common Book, however, are just the beginning. Active engagement at UCLA and within our larger community will be a critical part of your learning and of your success at UCLA and beyond. There are several avenues for involvement and endless ways to shape your experience at UCLA.

I encourage you to make the most of every opportunity UCLA offers as you continue on your path toward engaged global citizenship.

Welcome to the Bruin family!

Sincerely,

Gene D. Block
Chancellor

# UCLA PRINCIPLES OF COMMUNITY

The University of California, Los Angeles (UCLA) is an institution that is firmly rooted in its land-grant mission of teaching, research, and public service. The campus community is committed to discovery and innovation, creative and collaborative achievements, debate and critical inquiry, in an open and inclusive environment that nurtures the growth and development of all faculty, students, administration and staff. These Principles of Community are vital for ensuring a welcoming and inclusive environment for all members of the campus community and for serving as a guide for our personal and collective behavior.

- We believe that diversity is critical to maintaining excellence in all of our endeavors.

- We seek to foster open-mindedness, understanding, compassion and inclusiveness among individuals and groups.

- We are committed to ensuring freedom of expression and dialogue, in a respectful and civil manner, on the spectrum of views held by our varied and diverse campus communities.

- We value differences as well as commonalities and promote respect in personal interactions.

- We affirm our responsibility for creating and fostering a respectful, cooperative, equitable and civil campus environment for our diverse campus communities.

- We strive to build a community of learning and fairness marked by mutual respect.

- We do not tolerate acts of discrimination, harassment, profiling or other conduct causing harm to individuals on the basis of expression of race, color, ethnicity, gender, age, disability, religious beliefs, political preference, sexual orientation, gender identity, citizenship, or national origin among other personal characteristics. Such conduct violates UCLA's Principles of Community and may result in imposition of sanctions according to campus policies governing the conduct of students, staff and faculty.

- We acknowledge that modern societies carry historical and divisive biases based on race, ethnicity, gender, age, disability, sexual orientation, and religion, and we seek to promote awareness and understanding through education and research and to mediate and resolve conflicts that arise from these biases in our communities.

*The "Principles of Community" statement was developed by the Chancellor's Advisory Group on Diversity, since renamed the UCLA Council on Diversity & Inclusion, which is comprised of representatives from administration, faculty, staff, students and alumni. For more information, or to download copies of the statement, please see www.diversity.ucla.edu.*

*May 2010 | Updated March 2011*

# Common Book Discussion Questions

The diversity you encounter as you become part of the Bruin community is one of our strengths, and we are committed to developing a community that values and learns from the richness of our experiences, histories, dreams, and contributions. The Common Book experience provides a great opportunity for reflection, conversation and learning about each other. As you read *Between the World and Me*, please consider the following introductory questions, created by members of our Faculty in Residence program. We encourage you to reflect on the questions and the issues raised, and prepare for enlightening conversations with other Bruins.

1.  Coates is careful to avoid assuming that whiteness is a given. Rather, he calls attention to the constructedness of race when he describes families and individuals who "believe themselves to be white" or children who are "raised to be white" (10). At the same time, whiteness is a powerful social force, a descriptor for a community of those who have "maximum power and minimum responsibility," those who have the power to take the lives of others without punishment (80). What role does race play in your self-understanding? How does your understanding of yourself and your identities connect to the social and historical consequences Coates discusses?

2.  Coates writes that ". . . race is the child of racism, not the father" (7). What does the author mean by this? How does this assertion compel us to think about the history of race and racism in the United States? How does this apparent reversal of common sense compel us to rethink the history of race and racism in the United States?

3.  Coates writes of schools that "were not concerned with curiosity. They were concerned with compliance" (26). How does the author see the education system as complicit with a power that continues to divide America into separate worlds? Do you have personal experience with a school that was or was not concerned with curiosity?

5.  What does Coates mean by "the Dream"? Why does he urge himself to be "wary of every Dream" (53)? What do you think the author means when he writes that "the Dreamers . . . would rather live white than live free" (143)? Against the Dream, what does it mean to be "conscious citizen[s] of the terrible world" (108)?

6.  What is Coates' definition of race on p. 115? Do you agree? What other populations might this definition apply to globally, beyond those in the United States? If race is not a biological reality, then what is it?

7.  In what ways does history, or the media, tell us who or what matters? Who counts and who does not? Give examples. As a member of the Bruin community, what is your role in shaping/affirming/complicating/confronting these messages?

BY TA-NEHISI COATES

*Between the World and Me*

*The Beautiful Struggle*

# Between the World and Me

# Between the World and Me

Ta-Nehisi Coates

SPIEGEL & GRAU

NEW YORK

*Between the World and Me* is a work of nonfiction. Some names and identifying details have been changed.

Published in the United States by Spiegel & Grau, an imprint of Random House, a division of Penguin Random House LLC, New York.

Spiegel & Grau and the House colophon are registered trademarks of Penguin Random House LLC.

The title of this work is drawn from the poem "Between the World and Me" by Richard Wright, from *White Man Listen!* copyright © 1957 by Richard Wright. Used by permission of John Hawkins & Associates, Inc., and the Estate of Richard Wright.

Grateful acknowledgment is made to the following for permission to reprint previously published material:

Chris Calhoun Agency: Excerpt from "Ka' Ba" by Amiri Baraka, copyright © Estate of Amiri Baraka. Reprinted by permission of the Chris Calhoun Agency.

John Hawkins & Associates, Inc., and the Estate of Richard Wright: Excerpt from "Between the World and Me" from *White Man Listen!* by Richard Wright, copyright © 1957 by Richard Wright. Reprinted by permission of John Hawkins & Associates, Inc., and the Estate of Richard Wright.

Sonia Sanchez: Excerpt from "Malcolm" from *Shake Loose My Skin* by Sonia Sanchez (Boston: Beacon Press, 1999), copyright © 1999 by Sonia Sanchez. Reprinted by permission of Sonia Sanchez.

ISBN 978-0-3995-9065-8
eBook ISBN 978-0-679-64598-6

Printed in the United States of America on acid-free paper

randomhousebooks.com
spiegelandgrau.com

10 9 8 7 6 5 4 3 2 1

Book design by Caroline Cunningham

For David and Kenyatta,

who believed

*And one morning while in the woods I stumbled suddenly*
    *upon the thing,*
*Stumbled upon it in a grassy clearing guarded by scaly oaks*
    *and elms*
*And the sooty details of the scene rose, thrusting themselves*
    *between the world and me. . . .*

—Richard Wright

# Between the World and Me

# I.

*Do not speak to me of martyrdom,*
*of men who die to be remembered*
*on some parish day.*
*I don't believe in dying*
*though, I too shall die.*
*And violets like castanets*
*will echo me.*

SONIA SANCHEZ

Son,

Last Sunday the host of a popular news show asked me what it meant to lose my body. The host was broadcasting from Washington, D.C., and I was seated in a remote studio on the far west side of Manhattan. A satellite closed the miles between us, but no machinery could close the gap between her world and the world for which I had been summoned to speak. When the host asked me about my body, her face faded from the screen, and was replaced by a scroll of words, written by me earlier that week.

The host read these words for the audience, and when she finished she turned to the subject of my body, although she did not mention it specifically. But by now I am accustomed to intelligent people asking about the condition of my body without realizing the nature of their request. Specifically, the host wished to know why I felt that white America's progress, or rather the progress of those Americans who believe that they are white, was built on looting and violence. Hearing this, I felt an old and indistinct sadness well up in me. The answer to this question is the record of the believers themselves. The answer is American history.

There is nothing extreme in this statement. Americans deify democracy in a way that allows for a dim awareness that they have, from time to time, stood in defiance of their God. But democracy is a forgiving God and America's heresies—torture, theft, enslavement—are so common among individuals and nations that none can declare themselves immune. In fact, Americans, in a real sense, have never betrayed their God. When Abraham Lincoln declared, in 1863, that the battle of Gettysburg must ensure "that government of the people, by the people, for the people, shall not perish from the earth," he was not merely being aspirational; at the onset of the Civil War, the United States of America had one of the highest rates of suffrage in the world. The question is not whether Lincoln truly meant "government of the people" but what our country has, throughout its history, taken the political term "people" to actually mean. In 1863 it did not mean your mother or your grandmother, and it did not mean you and me. Thus America's problem is not its betrayal of "government of the people," but the means by which "the people" acquired their names.

This leads us to another equally important ideal, one

that Americans implicitly accept but to which they make no conscious claim. Americans believe in the reality of "race" as a defined, indubitable feature of the natural world. Racism—the need to ascribe bone-deep features to people and then humiliate, reduce, and destroy them—inevitably follows from this inalterable condition. In this way, racism is rendered as the innocent daughter of Mother Nature, and one is left to deplore the Middle Passage or the Trail of Tears the way one deplores an earthquake, a tornado, or any other phenomenon that can be cast as beyond the handiwork of men.

But race is the child of racism, not the father. And the process of naming "the people" has never been a matter of genealogy and physiognomy so much as one of hierarchy. Difference in hue and hair is old. But the belief in the preeminence of hue and hair, the notion that these factors can correctly organize a society and that they signify deeper attributes, which are indelible—this is the new idea at the heart of these new people who have been brought up hopelessly, tragically, deceitfully, to believe that they are white.

These new people are, like us, a modern invention. But unlike us, their new name has no real meaning divorced from the machinery of criminal power. The new people were something else before they were white—Catholic, Corsican, Welsh, Mennonite, Jewish—and if all our national hopes have any fulfillment, then they will have to be something else again. Perhaps they will truly become American and create a nobler basis for their myths. I cannot call it. As for now, it must be said that the process of washing the disparate tribes white, the elevation of the belief in being white, was not achieved through wine tastings and ice cream socials, but rather through the pillaging of life, liberty, labor, and land; through the flaying of backs; the chaining of limbs; the strangling of dissidents; the destruction of families; the rape of mothers; the sale of children; and various other acts meant, first and foremost, to deny you and me the right to secure and govern our own bodies.

The new people are not original in this. Perhaps there has been, at some point in history, some great power whose elevation was exempt from the violent exploitation of other human bodies. If there has been, I have yet to discover it. But this banality of violence can never excuse America, because America makes no claim to the banal. America believes itself exceptional, the greatest and noblest nation ever to exist, a lone champion standing between the white city of democracy and the terrorists, despots, barbarians, and other enemies of civilization. One cannot, at once, claim to be superhuman and then plead mortal error. I propose to take our countrymen's claims of American exceptionalism seriously, which is to say I propose subjecting our country to an exceptional moral standard. This is difficult because there exists, all around us, an apparatus urging us to accept American innocence at face value and not to inquire too much. And it is so easy to look away, to live with the fruits of our history and to ignore the great evil done in all of our names. But you and I have never truly had that luxury. I think you know.

I write you in your fifteenth year. I am writing you because this was the year you saw Eric Garner choked to death for selling cigarettes; because you know now that Renisha McBride was shot for seeking help, that John Crawford was shot down for browsing in a department store. And you have seen men in uniform drive by and murder Tamir Rice, a twelve-year-old child whom they were oath-bound to protect. And you have seen men in the same uniforms pummel Marlene Pinnock, someone's grandmother, on the side of a road. And you know now, if you did not before, that the police departments of your country have been endowed with the authority to destroy your body. It does not matter if the destruction is the result of an unfortunate overreaction. It does not matter if it originates in a misunderstanding. It does not matter if the destruction springs from a foolish policy. Sell cigarettes without the proper authority and your body can be destroyed. Resent the people trying to entrap your body and it can be destroyed. Turn into a dark stairwell and your body can be destroyed. The destroyers will rarely be held accountable. Mostly they will receive pensions. And destruction is merely the superlative form of a dominion whose prerogatives include friskings, detainings, beatings, and humiliations. All of this is common to black people. And all of this is old for black people. No one is held responsible.

There is nothing uniquely evil in these destroyers or even in this moment. The destroyers are merely men enforcing the whims of our country, correctly interpreting its heritage and legacy. It is hard to face this. But all our phrasing—race relations, racial chasm, racial justice, racial profiling, white privilege, even white supremacy—serves to obscure that racism is a visceral experience, that it dislodges brains, blocks airways, rips muscle, extracts organs, cracks bones, breaks teeth. You must never look away from this. You must always remember that the sociology, the history, the economics, the graphs, the charts, the regressions all land, with great violence, upon the body.

That Sunday, with that host, on that news show, I tried to explain this as best I could within the time allotted. But at the end of the segment, the host flashed a widely shared picture of an eleven-year-old black boy tearfully hugging a white police officer. Then she asked me about "hope." And I knew then that I had failed. And I remembered that I had expected to fail. And I wondered again at the indistinct sadness welling up in me. Why exactly was I sad? I came out of the studio and walked for a while. It was a calm December day. Families, believing themselves white, were out on the streets. Infants, raised to be white, were bundled in strollers. And I was sad for these people, much as I was sad for the host and sad for all the people out there watching and reveling in a specious hope. I realized then why I was sad. When the journalist asked me about my body, it was like she was asking me to awaken her from the most gorgeous dream. I have seen that dream all my life. It is perfect houses with nice lawns. It is Memorial Day cookouts, block associations, and driveways. The Dream is treehouses and the Cub Scouts. The Dream smells like peppermint but tastes like strawberry shortcake. And for so long I have wanted to escape into the Dream, to fold my country over my head like a blanket. But this has never been an option because the Dream rests on our backs, the bedding made from our bodies. And knowing this, knowing that the Dream persists by warring with the known world, I was sad for the host, I was sad for all those families, I was sad for my country, but above all, in that moment, I was sad for you.

That was the week you learned that the killers of Michael Brown would go free. The men who had left his body in the street like some awesome declaration of their inviolable power would never be punished. It was not my expectation that anyone would ever be punished. But you were young and still believed. You stayed up till 11 P.M. that night, waiting for the announcement of an indictment, and when instead it was announced that there was none you said, "I've got to go," and you went into your room, and I heard you crying. I came in five minutes after, and I didn't hug you, and I didn't comfort you, because I thought it would be wrong to comfort you. I did not tell you that it would be okay, because I have never believed it would be okay. What I told you is what your grandparents tried to tell me: that this is your country, that this is your world, that this is your body, and you must find some way to live within the all of it. I tell you now that the question of how one should live within a black body, within a country lost in the Dream, is the question of my life, and the pursuit of this question, I have found, ultimately answers itself.

This must seem strange to you. We live in a "goal-oriented" era. Our media vocabulary is full of hot takes, big ideas, and grand theories of everything. But some time ago I rejected magic in all its forms. This rejection was a gift from your grandparents, who never tried to console me with ideas of an afterlife and were skeptical of preordained American glory. In accepting both the chaos of history and the fact of my total end, I was freed to truly consider how I wished to live—specifically, how do I live free in this black body? It is a profound question because America understands itself as God's handiwork, but the black body is the clearest evidence that America is the work of men. I have asked the question through my reading and writings, through the music of my youth, through arguments with your grandfather, with your mother, your aunt Janai, your uncle Ben. I have searched for answers in nationalist myth, in classrooms, out on the streets, and on other continents. The question is unanswerable, which is not to say futile. The greatest reward of this constant interrogation, of confrontation with the brutality of my country, is that it has freed me from ghosts and girded me against the sheer terror of disembodiment.

And I am afraid. I feel the fear most acutely whenever you leave me. But I was afraid long before you, and in this I was unoriginal. When I was your age the only people I knew were black, and all of them were powerfully, adamantly, dangerously afraid. I had seen this fear all my young life, though I had not always recognized it as such.

It was always right in front of me. The fear was there in the extravagant boys of my neighborhood, in their large rings and medallions, their big puffy coats and full-length fur-collared leathers, which was their armor against their world. They would stand on the corner of Gwynn Oak and Liberty, or Cold Spring and Park Heights, or outside Mondawmin Mall, with their hands dipped in Russell sweats. I think back on those boys now and all I see is fear, and all I see is them girding themselves against the ghosts of the bad old days when the Mississippi mob gathered 'round their grandfathers so that the branches of the black body might be torched, then cut away. The fear lived on in their practiced bop, their slouching denim, their big T-shirts, the calculated angle of their baseball caps, a catalog of behaviors and garments enlisted to inspire the belief that these boys were in firm possession of everything they desired.

I saw it in their customs of war. I was no older than five, sitting out on the front steps of my home on Woodbrook Avenue, watching two shirtless boys circle each other close and buck shoulders. From then on, I knew that there was a ritual to a street fight, bylaws and codes that, in their very need, attested to all the vulnerability of the black teenage bodies.

I heard the fear in the first music I ever knew, the music that pumped from boom boxes full of grand boast and bluster. The boys who stood out on Garrison and Liberty up on Park Heights loved this music because it told them, against all evidence and odds, that they were masters of their own lives, their own streets, and their own bodies. I saw it in the girls, in their loud laughter, in their gilded bamboo earrings that announced their names thrice over. And I saw it in their brutal language and hard gaze, how they would cut you with their eyes and destroy you with their words for the sin of playing too much. "Keep my name out your mouth," they would say. I would watch them after school, how they squared off like boxers, vaselined up, earrings off, Reeboks on, and leaped at each other.

I felt the fear in the visits to my Nana's home in Philadelphia. You never knew her. I barely knew her, but what I remember is her hard manner, her rough voice. And I knew that my father's father was dead and that my uncle Oscar was dead and that my uncle David was dead and that each of these instances was unnatural. And I saw it in my own father, who loves you, who counsels you, who slipped me money to care for you. My father was so very afraid. I felt it in the sting of his black leather belt, which he applied with more anxiety than anger, my father who beat me as if someone might steal me away, because that is exactly what was happening all around us. Everyone had lost a child, somehow, to the streets, to jail, to drugs, to guns. It was said that these lost girls were sweet as honey and would not hurt a fly. It was said that these lost boys had just received a GED and had begun to turn their lives around. And now they were gone, and their legacy was a great fear.

Have they told you this story? When your grandmother was sixteen years old a young man knocked on her door. The young man was your Nana Jo's boyfriend. No one else was home. Ma allowed this young man to sit and wait until your Nana Jo returned. But your great-grandmother got there first. She asked the young man to leave. Then she beat your grandmother terrifically, one last time, so that she might remember how easily she could lose her body. Ma never forgot. I remember her clutching my small hand tightly as we crossed the street. She would tell me that if I ever let go and were killed by an onrushing car, she would beat me back to life. When I was six, Ma and Dad took me to a local park. I slipped from their gaze and found a playground. Your grandparents spent anxious minutes looking for me. When they found me, Dad did what every parent I knew would have done—he reached for his belt. I remember watching him in a kind of daze, awed at the distance between punishment and offense. Later, I would hear it in Dad's voice—"Either I can beat him, or the police." Maybe that saved me. Maybe it didn't. All I know is, the violence rose from the fear like smoke from a fire, and I cannot say whether that violence, even administered in fear and love, sounded the alarm or choked us at the exit. What I know is that fathers who slammed their teenage boys for sass would then release them to streets where their boys employed, and were subject to, the same justice. And I knew mothers who belted their girls, but the belt could not save these girls from drug dealers twice their age. We, the children, employed our darkest humor to cope. We stood in the alley where we shot basketballs through hollowed crates and cracked jokes on the boy whose mother wore him out with a beating in front of his entire fifth-grade class. We sat on the number five bus, headed downtown, laughing at some girl whose mother was known to reach for anything—cable wires, extension cords, pots, pans. We were laughing, but I know that we were afraid of those who loved us most. Our parents resorted to the lash the way flagellants in the plague years resorted to the scourge.

To be black in the Baltimore of my youth was to be naked before the elements of the world, before all the guns, fists, knives, crack, rape, and disease. The nakedness is not an error, nor pathology. The nakedness is the correct and intended result of policy, the predictable upshot of people forced for centuries to live under fear. The law did not protect us. And now, in your time, the law has become an excuse for stopping and frisking you, which is to say, for furthering the assault on your body. But a society that protects some people through a safety net of schools, government-backed home loans, and ancestral wealth but can only protect you with the club of criminal justice has either failed at enforcing its good intentions or has succeeded at something much darker. However you call it, the result was our infirmity before the criminal forces of the world. It does not matter if the agent of those forces is white or black—what matters is our condition, what matters is the system that makes your body breakable.

The revelation of these forces, a series of great changes, has unfolded over the course of my life. The changes are still unfolding and will likely continue until I die. I was eleven years old, standing out in the parking lot in front of the 7-Eleven, watching a crew of older boys standing near the street. They yelled and gestured at . . . who? . . . another boy, young, like me, who stood there, almost smiling, gamely throwing up his hands. He had already learned the lesson he would teach me that day: that his body was in constant jeopardy. Who knows what brought him to that knowledge? The projects, a drunken stepfather, an older brother concussed by police, a cousin pinned in the city jail. That he was outnumbered did not matter because the whole world had outnumbered him long ago, and what do numbers matter? This was a war for the possession of his body and that would be the war of his whole life.

I stood there for some seconds, marveling at the older boys' beautiful sense of fashion. They all wore ski jackets, the kind which, in my day, mothers put on layaway in September, then piled up overtime hours so as to have the thing wrapped and ready for Christmas. I focused in on a light-skinned boy with a long head and small eyes. He was scowling at another boy, who was standing close to me. It was just before three in the afternoon. I was in sixth grade. School had just let out, and it was not yet the fighting weather of early spring. What was the exact problem here? Who could know?

The boy with the small eyes reached into his ski jacket and pulled out a gun. I recall it in the slowest motion, as though in a dream. There the boy stood, with the gun brandished, which he slowly untucked, tucked, then untucked once more, and in his small eyes I saw a surging rage that could, in an instant, erase my body. That was 1986. That year I felt myself to be drowning in the news reports of murder. I was aware that these murders very often did not land upon the intended targets but fell upon great-aunts, PTA mothers, overtime uncles, and joyful children—fell upon them random and relentless, like great sheets of rain. I knew this in theory but could not understand it as fact until the boy with the small eyes stood across from me holding my entire body in his small hands. The boy did not shoot. His friends pulled him back. He did not need to shoot. He had affirmed my place in the order of things. He had let it be known how easily I could be selected. I took the subway home that day, processing the episode all alone. I did not tell my parents. I did not tell

my teachers, and if I told my friends I would have done so
with all the excitement needed to obscure the fear that
came over me in that moment.

I remember being amazed that death could so easily rise
up from the nothing of a boyish afternoon, billow up like
fog. I knew that West Baltimore, where I lived; that the
north side of Philadelphia, where my cousins lived; that
the South Side of Chicago, where friends of my father
lived, comprised a world apart. Somewhere out there beyond the firmament, past the asteroid belt, there were
other worlds where children did not regularly fear for
their bodies. I knew this because there was a large television resting in my living room. In the evenings I would sit
before this television bearing witness to the dispatches
from this other world. There were little white boys with
complete collections of football cards, and their only want
was a popular girlfriend and their only worry was poison
oak. That other world was suburban and endless, organized
around pot roasts, blueberry pies, fireworks, ice cream sun-
daes, immaculate bathrooms, and small toy trucks that
were loosed in wooded backyards with streams and glens.
Comparing these dispatches with the facts of my native
world, I came to understand that my country was a galaxy,
and this galaxy stretched from the pandemonium of West
Baltimore to the happy hunting grounds of *Mr. Belvedere*. I
obsessed over the distance between that other sector of
space and my own. I knew that my portion of the American galaxy, where bodies were enslaved by a tenacious

gravity, was black and that the other, liberated portion was not. I knew that some inscrutable energy preserved the breach. I felt, but did not yet understand, the relation between that other world and me. And I felt in this a cosmic injustice, a profound cruelty, which infused an abiding, irrepressible desire to unshackle my body and achieve the velocity of escape.

Do you ever feel that same need? Your life is so very different from my own. The grandness of the world, the real world, the whole world, is a known thing for you. And you have no need of dispatches because you have seen so much of the American galaxy and its inhabitants—their homes, their hobbies—up close. I don't know what it means to grow up with a black president, social networks, omnipresent media, and black women everywhere in their natural hair. What I know is that when they loosed the killer of Michael Brown, you said, "I've got to go." And that cut me because, for all our differing worlds, at your age my feeling was exactly the same. And I recall that even then I had not yet begun to imagine the perils that tangle us. You still believe the injustice was Michael Brown. You have not yet grappled with your own myths and narratives and discovered the plunder everywhere around us.

Before I could discover, before I could escape, I had to survive, and this could only mean a clash with the streets, by which I mean not just physical blocks, nor simply the people packed into them, but the array of lethal puzzles and strange perils that seem to rise up from the asphalt itself. The streets transform every ordinary day into a series of trick questions, and every incorrect answer risks a beat-down, a shooting, or a pregnancy. No one survives un-scathed. And yet the heat that springs from the constant danger, from a lifestyle of near-death experience, is thrill-ing. This is what the rappers mean when they pronounce themselves addicted to "the streets" or in love with "the game." I imagine they feel something akin to parachutists, rock climbers, BASE jumpers, and others who choose to live on the edge. Of course we chose nothing. And I have never believed the brothers who claim to "run," much less "own," the city. We did not design the streets. We do not fund them. We do not preserve them. But I was there, nevertheless, charged like all the others with the protec-tion of my body.

The crews, the young men who'd transmuted their fear into rage, were the greatest danger. The crews walked the blocks of their neighborhood, loud and rude, because it was only through their loud rudeness that they might feel any sense of security and power. They would break your jaw, stomp your face, and shoot you down to feel that power, to revel in the might of their own bodies. And their wild reveling, their astonishing acts made their names ring out. Reps were made, atrocities recounted. And so in my Baltimore it was known that when Cherry Hill rolled through you rolled the other way, that North and Pulaski was not an intersection but a hurricane, leaving only splin-ters and shards in its wake. In that fashion, the security of these neighborhoods flowed downward and became the security of the bodies living there. You steered clear of Jo-Jo, for instance, because he was cousin to Keon, the don of Murphy Homes. In other cities, indeed in other Baltimores, the neighborhoods had other handles and the boys went by other names, but their mission did not change: prove the inviolability of their block, of their bodies, through their power to crack knees, ribs, and arms. This practice was so common that today you can approach any black person raised in the cities of that era and they can tell you which crew ran which hood in their city, and they can tell you the names of all the captains and all their cousins and offer an anthology of all their exploits.

To survive the neighborhoods and shield my body, I learned another language consisting of a basic complement of head nods and handshakes. I memorized a list of prohibited blocks. I learned the smell and feel of fighting weather. And I learned that "Shorty, can I see your bike?" was never a sincere question, and "Yo, you was messing with my cousin" was neither an earnest accusation nor a misunderstanding of the facts. These were the summonses that you answered with your left foot forward, your right foot back, your hands guarding your face, one slightly lower than the other, cocked like a hammer. Or they were answered by breaking out, ducking through alleys, cutting through backyards, then bounding through the door past your kid brother into your bedroom, pulling the tool out of your lambskin or from under your mattress or out of your Adidas shoebox, then calling up your own cousins (who really aren't) and returning to that same block, on that same day, and to that same crew, hollering out, "Yeah, nigger, what's up now?" I recall learning these laws clearer than I recall learning my colors and shapes, because these laws were essential to the security of my body.

I think of this as a great difference between us. You have some acquaintance with the old rules, but they are not as essential to you as they were to me. I am sure that you have had to deal with the occasional roughneck on the subway or in the park, but when I was about your age, each day, fully one-third of my brain was concerned with who I was walking to school with, our precise number, the manner of our walk, the number of times I smiled, who or what I smiled at, who offered a pound and who did not—all of which is to say that I practiced the culture of the streets, a culture concerned chiefly with securing the body. I do not long for those days. I have no desire to make you "tough" or "street," perhaps because any "toughness" I garnered came reluctantly. I think I was always, somehow, aware of the price. I think I somehow knew that that third of my brain should have been concerned with more beautiful things. I think I felt that something out there, some force, nameless and vast, had robbed me of . . . what? Time? Experience? I think you know something of what that third could have done, and I think that is why you may feel the need for escape even more than I did. You have seen all the wonderful life up above the tree-line, yet you under-

stand that there is no real distance between you and Trayvon Martin, and thus Trayvon Martin must terrify you in a
way that he could never terrify me. You have seen so
much more of all that is lost when they destroy your body.

The streets were not my only problem. If the streets
shackled my right leg, the schools shackled my left. Fail to
comprehend the streets and you gave up your body now.
But fail to comprehend the schools and you gave up your
body later. I suffered at the hands of both, but I resent the
schools more. There was nothing sanctified about the laws
of the streets—the laws were amoral and practical. You
rolled with a posse to the party as sure as you wore boots
in the snow, or raised an umbrella in the rain. These were
rules aimed at something obvious—the great danger that
haunted every visit to Shake & Bake, every bus ride downtown. But the laws of the schools were aimed at something
distant and vague. What did it mean to, as our elders told
us, "grow up and be somebody"? And what precisely did
this have to do with an education rendered as rote discipline? To be educated in my Baltimore mostly meant
always packing an extra number 2 pencil and working quietly. Educated children walked in single file on the right
side of the hallway, raised their hands to use the lavatory,
and carried the lavatory pass when en route. Educated
children never offered excuses—certainly not childhood
itself. The world had no time for the childhoods of black
boys and girls. How could the schools? Algebra, Biology,
and English were not subjects so much as opportunities to

better discipline the body, to practice writing between the lines, copying the directions legibly, memorizing theorems extracted from the world they were created to represent. All of it felt so distant to me. I remember sitting in my seventh-grade French class and not having any idea why I was there. I did not know any French people, and nothing around me suggested I ever would. France was a rock rotating in another galaxy, around another sun, in another sky that I would never cross. Why, precisely, was I sitting in this classroom?

The question was never answered. I was a curious boy, but the schools were not concerned with curiosity. They were concerned with compliance. I loved a few of my teachers. But I cannot say that I truly believed any of them. Some years after I'd left school, after I'd dropped out of college, I heard a few lines from Nas that struck me:

*Ecstasy, coke, you say it's love, it is poison*
*Schools where I learn they should be burned, it is poison*

That was exactly how I felt back then. I sensed the schools were hiding something, drugging us with false morality so that we would not see, so that we did not ask: Why—for us and only us—is the other side of free will and free spirits an assault upon our bodies? This is not a hyperbolic concern. When our elders presented school to us, they did not present it as a place of high learning but as a means of escape from death and penal warehousing.

Fully 60 percent of all young black men who drop out of high school will go to jail. This should disgrace the country. But it does not, and while I couldn't crunch the numbers or plumb the history back then, I sensed that the fear that marked West Baltimore could not be explained by the schools. Schools did not reveal truths, they concealed them. Perhaps they must be burned away so that the heart of this thing might be known.

Unfit for the schools, and in good measure wanting to be unfit for them, and lacking the savvy I needed to master the streets, I felt there could be no escape for me or, honestly, anyone else. The fearless boys and girls who would knuckle up, call on cousins and crews, and, if it came to it, pull guns seemed to have mastered the streets. But their knowledge peaked at seventeen, when they ventured out of their parents' homes and discovered that America had guns and cousins, too. I saw their futures in the tired faces of mothers dragging themselves onto the 28 bus, swatting and cursing at three-year-olds; I saw their futures in the men out on the corner yelling obscenely at some young girl because she would not smile. Some of them stood outside liquor stores waiting on a few dollars for a bottle. We would hand them a twenty and tell them to keep the change. They would dash inside and return with Red Bull, Mad Dog, or Cisco. Then we would walk to the house of someone whose mother worked nights, play "Fuck tha Police," and drink to our youth. We could not get out. The ground we walked was trip-wired. The air we breathed was toxic. The water stunted our growth. We could not get out.

A year after I watched the boy with the small eyes pull out a gun, my father beat me for letting another boy steal from me. Two years later, he beat me for threatening my ninth-grade teacher. Not being violent enough could cost me my body. Being too violent could cost me my body. We could not get out. I was a capable boy, intelligent, well-liked, but powerfully afraid. And I felt, vaguely, wordlessly, that for a child to be marked off for such a life, to be forced to live in fear was a great injustice. And what was the source of this fear? What was hiding behind the smoke screen of streets and schools? And what did it mean that number 2 pencils, conjugations without context, Pythagorean theorems, handshakes, and head nods were the difference between life and death, were the curtains drawing down between the world and me?

I could not retreat, as did so many, into the church and its mysteries. My parents rejected all dogmas. We spurned the holidays marketed by the people who wanted to be white. We would not stand for their anthems. We would not kneel before their God. And so I had no sense that any just God was on my side. "The meek shall inherit the earth" meant nothing to me. The meek were battered in West Baltimore, stomped out at Walbrook Junction, bashed up on Park Heights, and raped in the showers of the city jail. My understanding of the universe was physical, and its moral arc bent toward chaos then concluded in a box.

That was the message of the small-eyed boy, untucking the piece—a child bearing the power to body and banish other children to memory. Fear ruled everything around me, and I knew, as all black people do, that this fear was connected to the Dream out there, to the unworried boys, to pie and pot roast, to the white fences and green lawns nightly beamed into our television sets.

But how? Religion could not tell me. The schools could not tell me. The streets could not help me see beyond the scramble of each day. And I was such a curious boy. I was raised that way. Your grandmother taught me to read when I was only four. She also taught me to write, by which I mean not simply organizing a set of sentences into a series of paragraphs, but organizing them as a means of investigation. When I was in trouble at school (which was quite often) she would make me write about it. The writing had to answer a series of questions: Why did I feel the need to talk at the same time as my teacher? Why did I not believe that my teacher was entitled to respect? How would I want someone to behave while I was talking? What would I do the next time I felt the urge to talk to my friends during a lesson? I have given you these same assignments. I gave them to you not because I thought they would curb your behavior—they certainly did not curb mine—but because these were the earliest acts of interrogation, of drawing myself into consciousness. Your grandmother was not teaching me how to behave in class. She was teaching me how to ruthlessly interrogate the subject that elicited the most sympathy and rationalizing—myself. Here was the lesson: I was not an innocent. My impulses were not filled with unfailing virtue. And feeling that I was as human as anyone, this must be true for other humans. If I was not innocent, then they were not innocent. Could this mix of motivation also affect the stories they tell? The cities they built? The country they claimed as given to them by God?

Now the questions began burning in me. The materials for research were all around me, in the form of books assembled by your grandfather. He was then working at Howard University as a research librarian in the Moorland-Spingarn Research Center, one of the largest collections of Africana in the world. Your grandfather loved books and loves them to this day, and they were all over the house, books about black people, by black people, for black people spilling off shelves and out of the living room, boxed up in the basement. Dad had been a local captain in the Black Panther Party. I read through all of Dad's books about the Panthers and his stash of old Party newspapers. I was attracted to their guns, because the guns seemed honest. The guns seemed to address this country, which invented the streets that secured them with despotic police, in its primary language—violence. And I compared the Panthers to the heroes given to me by the schools, men and women who struck me as ridiculous and contrary to everything I knew.

Every February my classmates and I were herded into

assemblies for a ritual review of the Civil Rights Movement. Our teachers urged us toward the example of freedom marchers, Freedom Riders, and Freedom Summers, and it seemed that the month could not pass without a series of films dedicated to the glories of being beaten on camera. The black people in these films seemed to love the worst things in life—love the dogs that rent their children apart, the tear gas that clawed at their lungs, the firehoses that tore off their clothes and tumbled them into the streets. They seemed to love the men who raped them, the women who cursed them, love the children who spat on them, the terrorists that bombed them. *Why are they showing this to us?* Why were only our heroes nonviolent? I speak not of the morality of nonviolence, but of the sense that blacks are in especial need of this morality. Back then all I could do was measure these freedom-lovers by what I knew. Which is to say, I measured them against children pulling out in the 7-Eleven parking lot, against parents wielding extension cords, and "Yeah, nigger, what's up now?" I judged them against the country I knew, which had acquired the land through murder and tamed it under slavery, against the country whose armies fanned out across the world to extend their dominion. The world, the real one, was civilization secured and ruled by savage means. How could the schools valorize men and women whose values society actively scorned? How could they send us out into the streets of Baltimore, knowing all that they were, and then speak of nonviolence?

I came to see the streets and the schools as arms of the same beast. One enjoyed the official power of the state while the other enjoyed its implicit sanction. But fear and violence were the weaponry of both. Fail in the streets and the crews would catch you slipping and take your body. Fail in the schools and you would be suspended and sent back to those same streets, where they would take your body. And I began to see these two arms in relation— those who failed in the schools justified their destruction in the streets. The society could say, "He should have stayed in school," and then wash its hands of him.

It does not matter that the "intentions" of individual educators were noble. Forget about intentions. What any institution, or its agents, "intend" for you is secondary. Our world is physical. Learn to play defense—ignore the head and keep your eyes on the body. Very few Americans will directly proclaim that they are in favor of black people being left to the streets. But a very large number of Americans will do all they can to preserve the Dream. No one directly proclaimed that schools were designed to sanctify failure and destruction. But a great number of educators spoke of "personal responsibility" in a country authored and sustained by a criminal irresponsibility. The point of this language of "intention" and "personal responsibility" is broad exoneration. Mistakes were made. Bodies were broken. People were enslaved. We meant well. We tried our best. "Good intention" is a hall pass through history, a sleeping pill that ensures the Dream.

An unceasing interrogation of the stories told to us by the schools now felt essential. It felt wrong not to ask why, and then to ask it again. I took these questions to my father, who very often refused to offer an answer, and instead referred me to more books. My mother and father were always pushing me away from secondhand answers—even the answers they themselves believed. I don't know that I have ever found any satisfactory answers of my own. But every time I ask it, the question is refined. That is the best of what the old heads meant when they spoke of being "politically conscious"—as much a series of actions as a state of being, a constant questioning, questioning as ritual, questioning as exploration rather than the search for certainty. Some things were clear to me: The violence that undergirded the country, so flagrantly on display during Black History Month, and the intimate violence of "Yeah, nigger, what's up now?" were not unrelated. And this violence was not magical, but was of a piece and by design.

But what exactly was the design? And why? I must know. I must get out ... but into what? I devoured the books because they were the rays of light peeking out from the doorframe, and perhaps past that door there was another world, one beyond the gripping fear that undergirded the Dream.

In this blooming consciousness, in this period of intense questioning, I was not alone. Seeds planted in the 1960s, forgotten by so many, sprung up from the ground and bore fruit. Malcolm X, who'd been dead for twenty-five years,

exploded out of the small gatherings of his surviving apos-
tles and returned to the world. Hip-hop artists quoted him
in lyrics, cut his speeches across the breaks, or flashed his
likeness in their videos. This was the early '90s. I was then
approaching the end of my time in my parents' home and
wondering about my life out there. If I could have chosen
a flag back then, it would have been embroidered with a
portrait of Malcolm X, dressed in a business suit, his tie
dangling, one hand parting a window shade, the other
holding a rifle. The portrait communicated everything
I wanted to be—controlled, intelligent, and beyond the
fear. I would buy tapes of Malcolm's speeches—"Message
to the Grassroots," "The Ballot or the Bullet"—down at
Everyone's Place, a black bookstore on North Avenue,
and play them on my Walkman. Here was all the angst I
felt before the heroes of February, distilled and quotable.
"Don't give up your life, preserve your life," he would say.
"And if you got to give it up, make it even-steven." This
was not boasting—it was a declaration of equality rooted
not in better angels or the intangible spirit but in the sanctity of the black body. You preserved your life because
your life, your body, was as good as anyone's, because your
blood was as precious as jewels, and it should never be sold
for magic, for spirituals inspired by the unknowable here-
after. You do not give your precious body to the billy
clubs of Birmingham sheriffs nor to the insidious gravity
of the streets. Black is beautiful—which is to say that the
black body is beautiful, that black hair must be guarded

against the torture of processing and lye, that black skin must be guarded against bleach, that our noses and mouths must be protected against modern surgery. We are all our beautiful bodies and so must never be prostrate before barbarians, must never submit our original self, our one of one, to defiling and plunder.

I loved Malcolm because Malcolm never lied, unlike the schools and their façade of morality, unlike the streets and their bravado, unlike the world of dreamers. I loved him because he made it plain, never mystical or esoteric, because his science was not rooted in the actions of spooks and mystery gods but in the work of the physical world. Malcolm was the first political pragmatist I knew, the first honest man I'd ever heard. He was unconcerned with making the people who believed they were white comfortable in their belief. If he was angry, he said so. If he hated, he hated because it was human for the enslaved to hate the enslaver, natural as Prometheus hating the birds. He would not turn the other cheek for you. He would not be a better man for you. He would not be your morality. Malcolm spoke like a man who was free, like a black man above the laws that proscribed our imagination. I identified with him. I knew that he had chafed against the schools, that he had almost been doomed by the streets. But even more I knew that he had found himself while studying in prison, and that when he emerged from the jails, he returned wielding some old power that made him speak as though his body were his own. "If you're black, you were born in jail," Malcolm said. And I felt the truth of this in the blocks I had to avoid, in the times of day when I must not be caught walking home from school, in my lack of control over my body. Perhaps I too might live free. Perhaps I too might wield the same old power that animated the ancestors, that lived in Nat Turner, Harriet Tubman, Nanny, Cudjoe, Malcolm X, and speak—no, act—as though my body were my own.

My reclamation would be accomplished, like Malcolm's, through books, through my own study and exploration. Perhaps I might write something of consequence someday. I had been reading and writing beyond the purview of the schools all my life. Already I was scribbling down bad rap lyrics and bad poetry. The air of that time was charged with the call for a return, to old things, to something essential, some part of us that had been left behind in the mad dash out of the past and into America.

This missing thing, this lost essence, explained the boys on the corner and "the babies having babies." It explained everything, from our cracked-out fathers to HIV to the bleached skin of Michael Jackson. The missing thing was related to the plunder of our bodies, the fact that any claim to ourselves, to the hands that secured us, the spine that braced us, and the head that directed us, was contestable. This was two years before the Million Man March. Almost every day I played Ice Cube's album *Death Certificate:* "Let me live my life, if we can no longer live our life, then let us give our life for the liberation and salvation of the black nation." I kept the Black Power episodes of *Eyes on*

*the Prize* in my weekly rotation. I was haunted by the shadow of my father's generation, by Fred Hampton and Mark Clark. I was haunted by the bodily sacrifice of Malcolm, by Attica and Stokely. I was haunted because I believed that we had left ourselves back there, undone by COINTELPRO and black flight and drugs, and now in the crack era all we had were our fears. Perhaps we should go back. That was what I heard in the call to "keep it real." Perhaps we should return to ourselves, to our own primordial streets, to our own ruggedness, to our own rude hair. Perhaps we should return to Mecca.


My only Mecca was, is, and shall always be Howard University. I have tried to explain this to you many times. You say that you hear me, that you understand, but I am not so sure that the force of my Mecca—The Mecca—can be translated into your new and eclectic tongue. I am not even sure that it should be. My work is to give you what I know of my own particular path while allowing you to walk your own. You can no more be black like I am black than I could be black like your grandfather was. And still, I maintain that even for a cosmopolitan boy like you, there is something to be found there—a base, even in these modern times, a port in the American storm. Surely I am biased by nostalgia and tradition. Your grandfather worked at Howard. Your uncles Damani and Menelik and your aunts Kris and Kelly graduated from there. I met your mother there, your uncle Ben, your aunt Kamilah and aunt Chana.

I was admitted to Howard University, but formed and shaped by The Mecca. These institutions are related but not the same. Howard University is an institution of higher education, concerned with the LSAT, magna cum laude, and Phi Beta Kappa. The Mecca is a machine, crafted to capture and concentrate the dark energy of all African peoples and inject it directly into the student body. The Mecca derives its power from the heritage of Howard University, which in Jim Crow days enjoyed a near-monopoly on black talent. And whereas most other historically black schools were scattered like forts in the great wilderness of the old Confederacy, Howard was in Washington, D.C.—Chocolate City—and thus in proximity to both federal power and black power. The result was an alumni and professorate that spanned genre and generation—Charles Drew, Amiri Baraka, Thurgood Marshall, Ossie Davis, Doug Wilder, David Dinkins, Lucille Clifton, Toni Morrison, Kwame Ture. The history, the location, the alumni combined to create The Mecca—the crossroads of the black diaspora.

I first witnessed this power out on the Yard, that communal green space in the center of the campus where the students gathered and I saw everything I knew of my black self multiplied out into seemingly endless variations. There were the scions of Nigerian aristocrats in their business suits giving dap to bald-headed Qs in purple windbreakers and tan Timbs. There were the high-yellow progeny of AME preachers debating the clerics of Ausar-Set. There were California girls turned Muslim, born anew, in hijab and long skirt. There were Ponzi schemers and Christian cultists, Tabernacle fanatics and mathematical geniuses. It was like listening to a hundred different renditions of "Redemption Song," each in a different color and key. And overlaying all of this was the history of Howard itself. I knew that I was literally walking in the footsteps of all the Toni Morrisons and Zora Neale Hurstons, of all the Sterling Browns and Kenneth Clarks, who'd come before. The Mecca—the vastness of black people across space-time—could be experienced in a twenty-minute walk across campus. I saw this vastness in the students chopping it up in front of the Frederick Douglass Memorial Hall, where Muhammad Ali had addressed their fathers and mothers in defiance of the Vietnam War. I saw its epic sweep in the students next to Ira Aldridge Theater, where Donny Hathaway had once sung, where Donald Byrd had once assembled his flock. The students came out with their saxophones, trumpets, and drums, played "My Favorite Things" or "Someday My Prince Will Come." Some of the other students were out on the grass in front of Alain Locke Hall, in pink and green, chanting, singing, stomping, clapping, stepping. Some of them came up from Tubman Quadrangle with their roommates and rope for Double Dutch. Some of them came down from Drew Hall, with their caps cocked and their backpacks slung through one arm, then fell into gorgeous ciphers of beatbox and rhyme. Some of the girls sat by the flagpole with bell hooks and Sonia Sanchez in their straw totes. Some of the boys, with their new Yoruba names, beseeched these girls by citing Frantz Fanon. Some of them studied Russian. Some of them worked in bone labs. They were Panamanian. They were Bajan. And some of them were from places I had never heard of. But all of them were hot and incredible, exotic even, though we hailed from the same tribe.

The black world was expanding before me, and I could see now that that world was more than a photonegative of that of the people who believe they are white. "White America" is a syndicate arrayed to protect its exclusive power to dominate and control our bodies. Sometimes this power is direct (lynching), and sometimes it is insidious (redlining). But however it appears, the power of domination and exclusion is central to the belief in being white, and without it, "white people" would cease to exist for want of reasons. There will surely always be people with straight hair and blue eyes, as there have been for all history. But some of these straight-haired people with blue eyes have been "black," and this points to the great difference between their world and ours. We did not choose our fences. They were imposed on us by Virginia planters obsessed with enslaving as many Americans as possible. They are the ones who came up with a one-drop rule that separated the "white" from the "black," even if it meant that their own blue-eyed sons would live under the lash.

The result is a people, black people, who embody all physical varieties and whose life stories mirror this physical range. Through The Mecca I saw that we were, in our own segregated body politic, cosmopolitans. The black diaspora was not just our own world but, in so many ways, the Western world itself.

Now, the heirs of those Virginia planters could never directly acknowledge this legacy or reckon with its power. And so that beauty that Malcolm pledged us to protect, black beauty, was never celebrated in movies, in television, or in the textbooks I'd seen as a child. Everyone of any import, from Jesus to George Washington, was white. This was why your grandparents banned Tarzan and the Lone Ranger and toys with white faces from the house. They were rebelling against the history books that spoke of black people only as sentimental "firsts"—first black five-star general, first black congressman, first black mayor—always presented in the bemused manner of a category of Trivial Pursuit. Serious history was the West, and the West was white. This was all distilled for me in a quote I once read from the novelist Saul Bellow. I can't remember where I read it, or when—only that I was already at Howard. "Who is the Tolstoy of the Zulus?" Bellow quipped. Tolstoy was "white," and so Tolstoy "mattered," like everything else that was white "mattered." And this view of things was connected to the fear that passed through the generations, to the sense of dispossession. We were black, beyond the visible spectrum, beyond civilization. Our history was inferior because we were inferior, which is to say our bodies were inferior. And our inferior bodies could not possibly be accorded the same respect as those that built the West. Would it not be better, then, if our bodies were civilized, improved, and put to some legitimate Christian use?

Contrary to this theory, I had Malcolm. I had my mother and father. I had my readings of every issue of *The Source* and *Vibe*. I read them not merely because I loved black music—I did—but because of the writing itself. Writers Greg Tate, Chairman Mao, dream hampton—barely older than me—were out there creating a new language, one that I intuitively understood, to analyze our art, our world. This was, in and of itself, an argument for the weight and beauty of our culture and thus of our bodies. And now each day, out on the Yard, I felt this weight and saw this beauty, not just as a matter of theory but also as demonstrable fact. And I wanted desperately to communicate this evidence to the world, because I felt—even if I did not completely know— that the larger culture's erasure of black beauty was intimately connected to the destruction of black bodies.

What was required was a new story, a new history told through the lens of our struggle. I had always known this, had heard the need for a new history in Malcolm, had seen the need addressed in my father's books. It was in the promise behind their grand titles—*Children of the Sun, Wonderful Ethiopians of the Ancient Cushite Empire, The African Origin of Civilization*. Here was not just our history but the history of the world, weaponized to our noble

ends. Here was the primordial stuff of our own Dream—
the Dream of a "black race"—of our own Tolstoys who
lived deep in the African past, where we authored operas,
pioneered secret algebra, erected ornate walls, pyramids,
colossi, bridges, roads, and all the inventions that I then
thought must qualify one's lineage for the ranks of civilization. They had their champions, and somewhere we must
have ours. By then I'd read Chancellor Williams, J. A.
Rogers, and John Jackson—writers central to the canon of
our new noble history. From them I knew that Mansa
Musa of Mali was black, and Shabaka of Egypt was black,
and Yaa Asantewaa of Ashanti was black—and "the black
race" was a thing I supposed existed from time immemo-
rial, a thing that was real and mattered.

When I came to Howard, Chancellor Williams's *Destruction of Black Civilization* was my Bible. Williams himself had taught at Howard. I read him when I was sixteen,
and his work offered a grand theory of multi-millennial
European plunder. The theory relieved me of certain
troubling questions—this is the point of nationalism—and
it gave me my Tolstoy. I read about Queen Nzinga, who
ruled in Central Africa in the sixteenth century, resisting
the Portuguese. I read about her negotiating with the
Dutch. When the Dutch ambassador tried to humiliate
her by refusing her a seat, Nzinga had shown her power by
ordering one of her advisers to all fours to make a human
chair of her body. That was the kind of power I sought,
and the story of our own royalty became for me a weapon.

My working theory then held all black people as kings in exile, a nation of original men severed from our original names and our majestic Nubian culture. Surely this was the message I took from gazing out on the Yard. Had any people, anywhere, ever been as sprawling and beautiful as us?

I needed more books. At Howard University, one of the greatest collections of books could be found in the Moorland-Spingarn Research Center, where your grandfather once worked. Moorland held archives, papers, collections, and virtually any book ever written by or about black people. For the most significant portion of my time at The Mecca, I followed a simple ritual. I would walk into the Moorland reading room and fill out three call slips for three different works. I would take a seat at one of these long tables. I would draw out my pen and one of my black-and-white composition books. I would open the books and read, while filling my composition books with notes on my reading, new vocabulary words, and sentences of my own invention. I would arrive in the morning and request, three call slips at a time, the works of every writer I had heard spoken of in classrooms or out on the Yard: Larry Neal, Eric Williams, George Padmore, Sonia Sanchez, Stanley Crouch, Harold Cruse, Manning Marable, Addison Gayle, Carolyn Rodgers, Etheridge Knight, Sterling Brown. I remember believing that the key to all life lay in articulating the precise difference between "the Black Aesthetic" and "Negritude." How, specifically, did

Europe underdevelop Africa? I must know. And if the Eighteenth Dynasty pharaohs were alive today, would they live in Harlem? I had to inhale all the pages.

I went into this investigation imagining history to be a unified narrative, free of debate, which, once uncovered, would simply verify everything I had always suspected. The smokescreen would lift. And the villains who manipulated the schools and the streets would be unmasked. But there was so much to know—so much geography to cover—Africa, the Caribbean, the Americas, the United States. And all of these areas had histories, sprawling literary canons, fieldwork, ethnographies. Where should I begin?

The trouble came almost immediately. I did not find a coherent tradition marching lockstep but instead factions, and factions within factions. Hurston battled Hughes, Du Bois warred with Garvey, Harold Cruse fought everyone. I felt myself at the bridge of a great ship that I could not control because C.L.R. James was a great wave and Basil Davidson was a swirling eddy, tossing me about. Things I believed merely a week earlier, ideas I had taken from one book, could be smashed to splinters by another. Had we retained any of our African inheritance? Frazier says it was all destroyed, and this destruction evidences the terribleness of our capturers. Herskovitz says it lives on, and this evidences the resilience of our African spirit. By my second year, it was natural for me to spend a typical day mediating between Frederick Douglass's integration into

America and Martin Delany's escape into nationalism. Perhaps they were somehow both right. I had come looking for a parade, for a military review of champions marching in ranks. Instead I was left with a brawl of ancestors, a herd of dissenters, sometimes marching together but just as often marching away from each other.

I would take breaks from my reading, walk out to the vendors who lined the streets, eat lunch on the Yard. I would imagine Malcolm, his body bound in a cell, studying the books, trading his human eyes for the power of flight. And I too felt bound by my ignorance, by the questions that I had not yet understood to be more than just means, by my lack of understanding, and by Howard itself. It was still a school, after all. I wanted to pursue things, to know things, but I could not match the means of knowing that came naturally to me with the expectations of professors. The pursuit of knowing was freedom to me, the right to declare your own curiosities and follow them through all manner of books. I was made for the library, not the classroom. The classroom was a jail of other people's interests. The library was open, unending, free. Slowly, I was discovering myself. The best parts of Malcolm pointed the way. Malcolm, always changing, always evolving toward some truth that was ultimately outside the boundaries of his life, of his body. I felt myself in motion, still directed toward the total possession of my body, but by some other route which I could not before then have imagined.

I was not searching alone. I met your uncle Ben at The

Mecca. He was, like me, from one of those cities where everyday life was so different than the Dream that it demanded an explanation. He came, like me, to The Mecca in search of the nature and origin of the breach. I shared with him a healthy skepticism and a deep belief that we could somehow read our way out. Ladies loved him, and what a place to be loved—for it was said, and we certainly believed it to be true, that nowhere on the Earth could one find a more beautiful assembly of women than on Howard University's Yard. And somehow even this was part of the search—the physical beauty of the black body was all our beauty, historical and cultural, incarnate. Your uncle Ben became a fellow traveler for life, and I discovered that there was something particular about journeying out with black people who knew the length of the road because they had traveled it too.

I would walk out into the city and find other searchers at lectures, book signings, and poetry readings. I was still writing bad poetry. I read this bad poetry at open mics in local cafés populated mostly by other poets who also felt the insecurity of their bodies. All of these poets were older and wiser than me, and many of them were well read, and they brought this wisdom to bear on me and my work. What did I mean, *specifically,* by the loss of my body? And if every black body was precious, a one of one, if Malcolm was correct and you must preserve your life, how could I see these precious lives as simply a collective mass, as the amorphous residue of plunder? How could I privilege the spectrum of dark energy over each particular ray of light? These were notes on how to write, and thus notes on how to think. The Dream thrives on generalization, on limiting the number of possible questions, on privileging immediate answers. The Dream is the enemy of all art, courageous thinking, and honest writing. And it became clear that this was not just for the dreams concocted by Americans to justify themselves but also for the dreams that I had conjured to replace them. I had thought that I must mirror the outside world, create a carbon copy of white claims to civilization. It was beginning to occur to me to question the logic of the claim itself. I had forgotten my own self-interrogations pushed upon me by my mother, or rather I had not yet apprehended their deeper, lifelong meaning. I was only beginning to learn to be wary of my own humanity, of my own hurt and anger—I didn't yet realize that the boot on your neck is just as likely to make you delusional as it is to ennoble.

The art I was coming to love lived in this void, in the not yet knowable, in the pain, in the question. The older poets introduced me to artists who pulled their energy from the void—Bubber Miley, Otis Redding, Sam and Dave, C. K. Williams, Carolyn Forché. The older poets were Ethelbert Miller, Kenneth Carroll, Brian Gilmore. It is important that I tell you their names, that you know that I have never achieved anything alone. I remember sitting with Joel Dias-Porter, who had not gone to Howard but whom I found at The Mecca, reviewing every line of

Robert Hayden's "Middle Passage." And I was stunned by how much Hayden managed to say without, seemingly, saying anything at all—he could bring forth joy and agony without literally writing the words, which formed as pictures and not slogans. Hayden imagined the enslaved, during the Middle Passage, from the perspective of the enslavers—a mind-trip for me, in and of itself; why should the enslaver be allowed to speak? But Hayden's poems did not speak. They conjured:

> *You cannot stare that hatred down*
> *or chain the fear that stalks the watches*

I was not in any slave ship. Or perhaps I was, because so much of what I'd felt in Baltimore, the sharp hatred, the immortal wish, and the timeless will, I saw in Hayden's work. And that was what I heard in Malcolm, but never like this—quiet, pure, and unadorned. I was learning the craft of poetry, which really was an intensive version of what my mother had taught me all those years ago—the craft of writing as the art of thinking. Poetry aims for an economy of truth—loose and useless words must be discarded, and I found that these loose and useless words were not separate from loose and useless thoughts. Poetry was not simply the transcription of notions—beautiful writing rarely is. I wanted to learn to write, which was ultimately, still, as my mother had taught me, a confrontation with my own innocence, my own rationalizations. Poetry was the processing of my thoughts until the slag of justification fell away and I was left with the cold steel truths of life.

These truths I heard in the works of other poets around the city. They were made of small hard things—aunts and uncles, smoke breaks after sex, girls on stoops drinking from mason jars. These truths carried the black body beyond slogans and gave it color and texture and thus reflected the spectrum I saw out on the Yard more than all of my alliterative talk of guns or revolutions or paeans to the lost dynasties of African antiquity. After these readings, I followed as the poets would stand out on U Street or repair to a café and argue about everything—books, politics, boxing. And their arguments reinforced the discordant tradition I'd found in Moorland, and I began to see discord, argument, chaos, perhaps even fear, as a kind of power. I was learning to live in the disquiet I felt in Moorland-Spingarn, in the mess of my mind. The gnawing discomfort, the chaos, the intellectual vertigo was not an alarm. It was a beacon.

It began to strike me that the point of my education was a kind of discomfort, was the process that would not award me my own especial Dream but would break all the dreams, all the comforting myths of Africa, of America, and everywhere, and would leave me only with humanity in all its terribleness. And there was so much terrible out there, even among us. You must understand this.

Back then, I knew, for instance, that just outside of Washington, D.C., there was a great enclave of black people who seemed, as much as anyone, to have seized control of their bodies. This enclave was Prince George's County—"PG County" to the locals—and it was, to my eyes, very rich. Its residents had the same homes, with the same backyards, with the same bathrooms, I'd seen in those televised dispatches. They were black people who elected their own politicians, but these politicians, I learned, superintended a police force as vicious as any in America. I had heard stories about PG County from the same poets who opened my world. These poets assured me that the PG County police were not police at all but privateers, gangsters, gunmen, plunderers operating under the color of law. They told me this because they wanted to protect my body. But there was another lesson here: To be black and beautiful was not a matter for gloating. Being black did not immunize us from history's logic or the lure of the Dream. The writer, and that was what I was becoming, must be wary of every Dream and every nation, even his own nation. Perhaps his own nation more than any other, precisely because it was his own.

I began to feel that something more than a national trophy case was needed if I was to be truly free, and for that I have the history department of Howard University to thank. My history professors thought nothing of telling me that my search for myth was doomed, that the stories I wanted to tell myself could not be matched to truths. Indeed, they felt it their duty to disabuse me of my weaponized history. They had seen so many Malcolmites before and were ready. Their method was rough and direct. Did black skin really convey nobility? Always? *Yes.* What about the blacks who'd practiced slavery for millennia and sold slaves across the Sahara and then across the sea? *Victims of a trick.* Would those be the same black kings who birthed all of civilization? Were they then both deposed masters of the galaxy and gullible puppets all at once? And what did I mean by "black"? *You know, black.* Did I think this a timeless category stretching into the deep past? *Yes?* Could it be supposed that simply because color was important to me, it had always been so?

I remember taking a survey class focusing on Central Africa. My professor, Linda Heywood, was slight and bespectacled, spoke with a high Trinidadian lilt that she employed like a hammer against young students like me who confused agitprop with hard study. There was nothing romantic about her Africa, or rather, there was nothing romantic in the sense that I conceived of it. And she took it back to the legacy of Queen Nzinga—my Tolstoy—the very same Nzinga whose life I wished to put in my trophy case. But when she told the story of Nzinga conducting negotiations upon the woman's back, she told it without any fantastic gloss, and it hit me hard as a sucker punch: Among the people in that room, all those centuries ago, my body, breakable at will, endangered in the streets, fearful in the schools, was not closest to the queen's but to her adviser's, who'd been broken down into a chair so that a queen, heir to everything she'd ever seen, could sit.

I took a survey of Europe post-1800. I saw black people, rendered through "white" eyes, unlike any I'd seen before—the black people looked regal and human. I remember the soft face of Alessandro de' Medici, the royal bearing of Bosch's black magi. These images, cast in the sixteenth and seventeenth centuries, were contrasted with those created after enslavement, the Sambo caricatures I had always known. What was the difference? In my survey course of America, I'd seen portraits of the Irish drawn in the same ravenous, lustful, and simian way. Perhaps there had been other bodies, mocked, terrorized, and insecure. Perhaps the Irish too had once lost their bodies. Perhaps being named "black" had nothing to do with any of this; perhaps being named "black" was just someone's name for being at the bottom, a human turned to object, object turned to pariah.

This heap of realizations was a weight. I found them physically painful and exhausting. True, I was coming to enjoy the dizziness, the vertigo that must come with any odyssey. But in those early moments, the unceasing contradictions sent me into a gloom. There was nothing holy or particular in my skin; I was black because of history and heritage. There was no nobility in falling, in being bound, in living oppressed, and there was no inherent meaning in black blood. Black blood wasn't black; black *skin* wasn't even black. And now I looked back on my need for a trophy case, on the desire to live by the standards of Saul Bellow, and I felt that this need was not an escape but fear again—fear that "they," the alleged authors and heirs of the universe, were right. And this fear ran so deep that we accepted their standards of civilization and humanity.

But not all of us. It must have been around that time that I discovered an essay by Ralph Wiley in which he responded to Bellow's quip. "Tolstoy is the Tolstoy of the Zulus," wrote Wiley. "Unless you find a profit in fencing off universal properties of mankind into exclusive tribal ownership." And there it was. I had accepted Bellow's premise. In fact, Bellow was no closer to Tolstoy than I was to Nzinga. And if I were closer it would be because I chose to be, not because of destiny written in DNA. My great error was not that I had accepted someone else's dream but that I had accepted the fact of dreams, the need for escape, and the invention of racecraft.

And still and all I knew that *we were* something, that we were a tribe—on one hand, invented, and on the other, no less real. The reality was out there on the Yard, on the first warm day of spring when it seemed that every sector, borough, affiliation, county, and corner of the broad diaspora had sent a delegate to the great world party. I remember those days like an OutKast song, painted in lust and joy. A baldhead in shades and a tank top stands across from Blackburn, the student center, with a long boa draping his muscular shoulders. A conscious woman, in stonewash with her dreads pulled back, is giving him the side-eye and laughing. I am standing outside the library debating the Republican takeover of Congress or the place of Wu-Tang

Clan in the canon. A dude in a Tribe Vibe T-shirt walks up, gives a pound, and we talk about the black bacchanals of the season—Freaknik, Daytona, Virginia Beach—and we wonder if this is the year we make the trip. It isn't. Because we have all we need out on the Yard. We are dazed here because we still remember the hot cities in which we were born, where the first days of spring were laced with fear. And now, here at The Mecca, we are without fear, we are the dark spectrum on parade.

These were my first days of adulthood, of living alone, of cooking for myself, of going and coming as I pleased, of my own room, of the chance of returning there, perhaps, with one of those beautiful women who were now everywhere around me. In my second year at Howard, I fell hard for a lovely girl from California who was then in the habit of floating over the campus in a long skirt and head wrap. I remember her large brown eyes, her broad mouth and cool voice. I would see her out on the Yard on those spring days, yell her name and then throw up my hands as though signaling a touchdown—but wider—like the "W" in "What up?" That was how we did it then. Her father was from Bangalore, and where was that? And what were the laws out there? I did not yet understand the import of my own questions. What I remember is my ignorance. I remember watching her eat with her hands and feeling wholly uncivilized with my fork. I remember wondering why she wore so many scarves. I remember her going to India for spring break and returning with a bindi on her head and photos of her smiling Indian cousins. I told her, "Nigga, you black" because that's all I had back then. But her beauty and stillness broke the balance in me. In my small apartment, she kissed me, and the ground opened up, swallowed me, buried me right there in that moment. How many awful poems did I write thinking of her? I know now what she was to me—the first glimpse of a space-bridge, a wormhole, a galactic portal off this bound and blind planet. She had seen other worlds, and she held the lineage of other worlds, spectacularly, in the vessel of her black body.

I fell again, a short time later and in similar fashion, for another girl, tall with long flowing dreadlocks. She was raised by a Jewish mother in a small, nearly all-white town in Pennsylvania, and now, at Howard, ranged between women and men, asserted this not just with pride but as though it were normal, *as though she were normal.* I know it's nothing to you now, but I was from a place—America—where cruelty toward humans who loved as their deepest instincts instructed was a kind of law. I was amazed. This was something black people did? Yes. And they did so much more. The girl with the long dreads lived in a house with a man, a Howard professor, who was married to a white woman. The Howard professor slept with men. His wife slept with women. And the two of them slept with each other. They had a little boy who must be off to college by now. "Faggot" was a word I had employed all my life. And now here they were, The Cabal, The Coven, The

Others, The Monsters, The Outsiders, The Faggots, The Dykes, dressed in all their human clothes. I am black, and have been plundered and have lost my body. But perhaps I too had the capacity for plunder, maybe I would take another human's body to confirm myself in a community. Perhaps I already had. Hate gives identity. The nigger, the fag, the bitch illuminate the border, illuminate what we ostensibly are not, illuminate the Dream of being white, of being a Man. We name the hated strangers and are thus confirmed in the tribe. But my tribe was shattering and reforming around me. I saw these people often, because they were family to someone whom I loved. Their ordinary moments—answering the door, cooking in the kitchen, dancing to Adina Howard—assaulted me and expanded my notion of the human spectrum. I would sit in the living room of that house, observing their private jokes, one part of me judging them, the other reeling from the changes.

She taught me to love in new ways. In my old house your grandparents ruled with the fearsome rod. I have tried to address you differently—an idea begun by seeing all the other ways of love on display at The Mecca. Here is how it started: I woke up one morning with a minor headache. With each hour the headache grew. I was walking to my job when I saw this girl on her way to class. I looked awful, and she gave me some Advil and kept going. By mid-afternoon I could barely stand. I called my supervisor. When he arrived I lay down in the stockroom, because I had no idea what else to do. I was afraid. I did not understand what was happening. I did not know whom to call. I was lying there simmering, half-awake, hoping to recover. My supervisor knocked on the door. Someone had come to see me. It was her. The girl with the long dreads helped me out and onto the street. She flagged down a cab. Halfway through the ride, I opened the door, with the cab in motion, and vomited in the street. But I remember her holding me there to make sure I didn't fall out and then holding me close when I was done. She took me to that house of humans, which was filled with all manner of love, put me in the bed, put *Exodus* on the CD player, and turned the volume down to a whisper. She left a bucket by the bed. She left a jug of water. She had to go to class. I slept. When she returned I was back in form. We ate. The girl with the long dreads who slept with whomever she chose, that being her own declaration of control over her body, was there. I grew up in a house drawn between love and fear. There was no room for softness. But this girl with the long dreads revealed something else— that love could be soft and understanding; that, soft or hard, love was an act of heroism.

And I could no longer predict where I would find my heroes. Sometimes I would walk with friends down to U Street and hang out at the local clubs. This was the era of Bad Boy and Biggie, "One More Chance" and "Hypnotize." I almost never danced, as much as I wanted to. I was crippled by some childhood fear of my own body. But I would watch how black people moved, how in these clubs they danced as though their bodies could do anything, and their bodies seemed as free as Malcolm's voice. On the outside black people controlled nothing, least of all the fate of their bodies, which could be commandeered by the police; which could be erased by the guns, which were so profligate; which could be raped, beaten, jailed. But in the clubs, under the influence of two-for-one rum and Cokes, under the spell of low lights, in thrall of hip-hop music, I felt them to be in total control of every step, every nod, every pivot.

All I then wanted was to write as those black people danced, with control, power, joy, warmth. I was in and out of classes at Howard. I felt that it was time to go, to declare myself a graduate of The Mecca, if not the university. I was publishing music reviews, articles, and essays in the local alternative newspaper, and this meant contact with more human beings. I had editors—more teachers—and these were the first white people I'd ever really known on any personal level. They defied my presumptions—they were afraid neither for me nor of me. Instead they saw in my unruly curiosity and softness something that was to be treasured and harnessed. And they gave me the art of journalism, a powerful technology for seekers. I reported on local D.C., and I found that people would tell me things, that the same softness that once made me a target now compelled people to trust me with their stories. This was incredible. I was barely out of the fog of childhood, where questions simply died in my head. Now I could call and ask people why a popular store closed, why a show had been canceled, why there were so many churches and so few supermarkets. Journalism gave me another tool of exploration, another way of unveiling the laws that bound my body. It was beginning to come together—even if I could not yet see what the "it" was.

In Moorland I could explore the histories and traditions. Out on the Yard, I could see these traditions in effect. And with journalism, I could directly ask people about the two—or about anything else I might wonder. So much of my life was defined by not knowing. Why did I live in a world where teenage boys stood in the parking lot of the 7-Eleven pulling out? Why was it normal for my father, like all the parents I knew, to reach for his belt? And why was life so different out there, in that other world past the asteroids? What did the people whose images were once beamed into my living room have that I did not?

The girl with the long dreads who changed me, whom I so wanted to love, she loved a boy about whom I think every day and about whom I expect to think every day for the rest of my life. I think sometimes that he was an invention, and in some ways he is, because when the young are killed, they are haloed by all that was possible, all that was plundered. But I know that I had love for this boy, Prince Jones, which is to say that I would smile whenever I saw him, for I felt the warmth when I was around him and was slightly sad when the time came to trade dap and for one of us to go. The thing to understand about Prince Jones is that he exhibited the whole of his given name. He was handsome. He was tall and brown, built thin and powerful like a wide receiver. He was the son of a prominent doctor. He was born-again, a state I did not share but respected. He was kind. Generosity radiated off of him, and he seemed to have a facility with everyone and everything. This can never be true, but there are people who pull the illusion off without effort, and Prince was one of them. I can only say what I saw, what I felt. There are people whom we do not fully know, and yet they live in a warm place within us, and when they are plundered, when they lose their bodies and the dark energy disperses, that place becomes a wound.

I fell in love at The Mecca one last time, lost my balance and all my boyhood confusion, under the spell of a girl from Chicago. This was your mother. I see us standing there with a group of friends in the living room of her home. I stood with a blunt in one hand and a beer in another. I inhaled, passed it off to this Chicago girl, and when I brushed her long elegant fingers, I shuddered a bit from the blast. She brought the blunt to her plum-painted lips, pulled, exhaled, then pulled the smoke back in. A week earlier I had kissed her, and now, watching this display of smoke and flame (and already feeling the effects), I was lost and running and wondering what it must be to embrace her, to be exhaled by her, to return to her, and leave her high.

She had never known her father, which put her in the company of the greater number of everyone I'd known. I felt then that these men—these "fathers"—were the greatest of cowards. But I also felt that the galaxy was playing with loaded dice, which ensured an excess of cowards in our ranks. The girl from Chicago understood this too, and she understood something more—that all are not equally robbed of their bodies, that the bodies of women are set out for pillage in ways I could never truly know. And she was the kind of black girl who'd been told as a child that she had better be smart because her looks wouldn't save her, and then told as a young woman that she was really pretty for a dark-skinned girl. And so there was, all about her, a knowledge of cosmic injustices, the same knowledge I'd glimpsed all those years ago watching my father reach for his belt, watching the suburban dispatches in my living room, watching the golden-haired boys with their toy trucks and football cards, and dimly perceiving the great barrier between the world and me.

Nothing between us was ever planned—not even you. We were both twenty-four years old when you were born, the normal age for most Americans, but among the class we soon found ourselves, we ranked as teenage parents. With a whiff of fear, we were very often asked if we planned to marry. Marriage was presented to us as a shield against other women, other men, or the corrosive monotony of dirty socks and dishwashing. But your mother and I knew too many people who'd married and abandoned each other for less. The truth of us was always that you were our ring. We'd summoned you out of ourselves, and you were not given a vote. If only for that reason, you deserved all the protection we could muster. Everything else was subordinate to this fact. If that sounds like a weight, it shouldn't. The truth is that I owe you everything I have. Before you, I had my questions but nothing beyond my own skin in the game, and that was really nothing at all because I was a young man, and not yet clear of my own human vulnerabilities. But I was grounded and domesticated by the plain fact that should I now go down, I would not go down alone.

This is what I told myself, at least. It was comforting to believe that the fate of my body and the bodies of my family were under my powers. "You will have to man up," we tell our sons. "Anyone can make a baby, but it takes a man to be a father." This is what they had told me all my life. It was the language of survival, a myth that helped us cope with the human sacrifice that finds us no matter our manhood. As though our hands were ever our own. As though plunder of dark energy was not at the heart of our galaxy. And the plunder was there, if I wished to see it.

One summer, I traveled out to Chicago to see your mother. I rode down the Dan Ryan with friends and beheld, for the first time, the State Street Corridor—a four-mile stretch of dilapidated public housing. There were projects all over Baltimore, but nothing so expansive as this. The housing occurred to me as a moral disaster not just for the people living there but for the entire region, the metropolis of commuters who drove by, each day, and with their quiet acquiescence tolerated such a thing. But there was so much more there in those projects than I was, even in all my curiosity, prepared to see.

Your maternal grandmother once visited us during the pregnancy. She must have been horrified. We were living in Delaware. We had almost no furniture. I had left Howard without a degree and was living on the impoverished wages of a freelance writer. On the last day of her visit, I drove your grandmother to the airport. Your mother was her only child, as you are my only child. And having watched you grow, I know that nothing could possibly be more precious to her. She said to me, "You take care of my daughter." When she got out of the car, my world had shifted. I felt that I had crossed some threshold, out of the foyer of my life and into the living room. Everything that was the past seemed to be another life. There was before you, and then there was after, and in this after, you were the God I'd never had. I submitted before your needs, and I knew then that I must survive for something more than survival's sake. I must survive for you.

You were born that August. I thought of the great spectrum of The Mecca—black people from Belize, black people with Jewish mothers, black people with fathers from Bangalore, black people from Toronto and Kingston, black people who spoke Russian, who spoke Spanish, who played Mongo Santamaría, who understood mathematics and sat up in bone labs, unearthing the mysteries of the enslaved. There was more out there than I had ever hoped for, and I wanted you to have it. I wanted you to know that the world in its entirety could never be found in the schools, alone, nor on the streets, alone, nor in the trophy case. I wanted you to claim the whole world, as it is. I wanted "Tolstoy is the Tolstoy of the Zulus" to immediately be obvious to you. And yet even in this cosmopolitan wish I felt the old power of ancestry, because I had come to knowledge at The Mecca that my ancestors made, and I was compelled toward The Mecca by the struggle that my ancestors made.

The Struggle is in your name, Samori—you were named for Samori Touré, who struggled against French colonizers for the right to his own black body. He died in captivity, but the profits of that struggle and others like it are ours, even when the object of our struggle, as is so often true, escapes our grasp. I learned this living among a people whom I would never have chosen, because the privileges of being black are not always self-evident. We are, as Derrick Bell once wrote, the "faces at the bottom of the well." But there really is wisdom down here, and that wisdom accounts for much of the good in my life. And my life down here accounts for you.

There was also wisdom in those streets. I think now of the old rule that held that should a boy be set upon in someone else's chancy hood, his friends must stand with him, and they must all take their beating together. I now know that within this edict lay the key to all living. None of us were promised to end the fight on our feet, fists raised to the sky. We could not control our enemies' number, strength, nor weaponry. Sometimes you just caught a bad one. But whether you fought or ran, you did it together, because that is the part that was in our control. What we must never do is willingly hand over our own bodies or the bodies of our friends. That was the wisdom: We knew we did not lay down the direction of the street, but despite that, we could—and must—fashion the way of our walk. And that is the deeper meaning of your name—that the struggle, in and of itself, has meaning.

That wisdom is not unique to our people, but I think it has special meaning to those of us born out of mass rape, whose ancestors were carried off and divided up into policies and stocks. I have raised you to respect every human being as singular, and you must extend that same respect into the past. Slavery is not an indefinable mass of flesh. It is a particular, specific enslaved woman, whose mind is active as your own, whose range of feeling is as vast as your own; who prefers the way the light falls in one particular spot in the woods, who enjoys fishing where the water eddies in a nearby stream, who loves her mother in her own complicated way, thinks her sister talks too loud, has a favorite cousin, a favorite season, who excels at dressmaking and knows, inside herself, that she is as intelligent and capable as anyone. "Slavery" is this same woman born in a world that loudly proclaims its love of freedom and inscribes this love in its essential texts, a world in which these same professors hold this woman a slave, hold her mother a slave, her father a slave, her daughter a slave, and when this woman peers back into the generations all she sees is the enslaved. She can hope for more. She can imagine some future for her grandchildren. But when she dies, the world—which is really the only world she can ever know—ends. For this woman, enslavement is not a parable. It is damnation. It is the never-ending night. And the length of that night is most of our history. Never forget that we were enslaved in this country longer than we have been free. Never forget that for 250 years black people were born into chains—whole generations followed by more generations who knew nothing but chains.

You must struggle to truly remember this past in all its nuance, error, and humanity. You must resist the common urge toward the comforting narrative of divine law, toward fairy tales that imply some irrepressible justice. The enslaved were not bricks in your road, and their lives were not chapters in your redemptive history. They were people turned to fuel for the American machine. Enslavement was not destined to end, and it is wrong to claim our present circumstance—no matter how improved—as the redemption for the lives of people who never asked for the posthumous, untouchable glory of dying for their children. Our triumphs can never compensate for this. Perhaps our triumphs are not even the point. Perhaps struggle is all we have because the god of history is an atheist, and nothing about his world is meant to be. So you must wake up every morning knowing that no promise is unbreakable, least of all the promise of waking up at all. This is not despair. These are the preferences of the universe itself: verbs over nouns, actions over states, struggle over hope.

The birth of a better world is not ultimately up to you, though I know, each day, there are grown men and women who tell you otherwise. The world needs saving precisely because of the actions of these same men and women. I am not a cynic. I love you, and I love the world, and I love it more with every new inch I discover. But you are a black boy, and you must be responsible for your body in a way that other boys cannot know. Indeed, you must be responsible for the worst actions of other black bodies, which, somehow, will always be assigned to you. And you must be responsible for the bodies of the powerful—the policeman who cracks you with a nightstick will quickly find his excuse in your furtive movements. And this is not reducible to just you—the women around you must be responsible for their bodies in a way that you never will know. You have to make your peace with the chaos, but you cannot lie. You cannot forget how much they took from us and how they transfigured our very bodies into sugar, tobacco, cotton, and gold.

## II.

*Our world is full of sound*
*Our world is more lovely than anyone's*
*tho we suffer, and kill each other*
*and sometimes fail to walk the air*

*We are beautiful people*
*with african imaginations*
*full of masks and dances and swelling chants*

*with african eyes, and noses, and arms,*
*though we sprawl in grey chains in a place*
*full of winters, when what we want is sun.*

AMIRI BARAKA

Shortly before you were born, I was pulled over by the PG County police, the same police that all the D.C. poets had warned me of. They approached on both sides of the car, shining their flashing lights through the windows. They took my identification and returned to the squad car. I sat there in terror. By then I had added to the warnings of my teachers what I'd learned about PG County through reporting and reading the papers. And so I knew that the PG County police had killed Elmer Clay Newman, then claimed he'd rammed his own head into the wall of a jail cell. And I knew that they'd shot Gary Hopkins and said he'd gone for an officer's gun. And I knew they had beaten Freddie McCollum half-blind and blamed it all on a collapsing floor. And I had read reports of these officers choking mechanics, shooting construction workers, slamming suspects through the glass doors of shopping malls.

And I knew that they did this with great regularity, as though moved by some unseen cosmic clock. I knew that they shot at moving cars, shot at the unarmed, shot through the backs of men and claimed that it had been they who'd been under fire. These shooters were investigated, exonerated, and promptly returned to the streets, where, so emboldened, they shot again. At that point in American history, no police department fired its guns more than that of Prince George's County. The FBI opened multiple investigations—sometimes in the same week. The police chief was rewarded with a raise. I replayed all of this sitting there in my car, in their clutches. Better to have been shot in Baltimore, where there was the justice of the streets and someone might call the killer to account. But these officers had my body, could do with that body whatever they pleased, and should I live to explain what they had done with it, this complaint would mean nothing. The officer returned. He handed back my license. He gave no explanation for the stop.

Then that September I picked up *The Washington Post* and saw that the PG County police had killed again. I could not help but think that this could have been me, and holding you—a month old by then—I knew that such loss would not be mine alone. I skimmed the headline—their atrocities seemed so common back then. The story spread into a second day, and reading slightly closer, I saw it was a Howard student who had been killed. I thought perhaps I knew him. But I paid it no further mind. Then on the third day a photo appeared with the story, and I glimpsed at and then focused on the portrait, and I saw him there. He was dressed in his formal clothes, as though it were his senior prom, and frozen in the amber of his youth. His face was lean, brown, and beautiful, and across that face, I saw the open, easy smile of Prince Carmen Jones.

I cannot remember what happened next. I think I stumbled back. I think I told your mother what I'd read. I think I called the girl with the long dreads and asked her if it could be true. I think she screamed. What I remember for sure is what I felt: rage and the old gravity of West Baltimore, the gravity that condemned me to the schools, the streets, the void. Prince Jones had made it through, and still they had taken him. And even though I already knew that I would never believe any account that justified this taking, I sat down to read the story. There were very few details. He had been shot by a PG County officer, not in PG County, not even in D.C., but somewhere in Northern Virginia. Prince had been driving to see his fiancée. He was killed yards from her home. The only witness to the killing of Prince Jones was the killer himself. The officer claimed that Prince had tried to run him over with his jeep, and I knew that the prosecutors would believe him.

Days later, your mother and I packed you into the car, drove down to Washington, left you with your aunt Kamilah, and went to the service for Prince at Rankin Chapel on Howard's campus, where I'd once sat amazed at the parade of activists and intellectuals—Joseph Lowery, Cornel West, Calvin Butts—who preached at that pulpit. I must have seen a great number of old friends there, though I cannot recall precisely who. What I remember is all the people who spoke of Prince's religious zeal, his abiding belief that Jesus was with him. I remember watching the president of the university stand and weep. I remember Dr. Mable Jones, Prince's mother, speaking of her son's death as a call to move from her comfortable suburban life into activism. I heard several people ask for forgiveness for the officer who'd shot Prince Jones down. I only vaguely recall my impressions of all this. But I know that I have always felt great distance from the grieving rituals of my people, and I must have felt it powerfully then. The need to forgive the officer would not have moved me, because even then, in some inchoate form, I knew that Prince was not killed by a single officer so much as he was murdered by his country and all the fears that have marked it from birth.

At this moment the phrase "police reform" has come into vogue, and the actions of our publicly appointed guardians have attracted attention presidential and pedestrian. You may have heard the talk of diversity, sensitivity training, and body cameras. These are all fine and applicable, but they understate the task and allow the citizens of this country to pretend that there is real distance between their own attitudes and those of the ones appointed to protect them. The truth is that the police reflect America in all of its will and fear, and whatever we might make of this country's criminal justice policy, it cannot be said that it was imposed by a repressive minority. The abuses that have followed from these policies—the sprawling carceral state, the random detention of black people, the torture of suspects—are the product of democratic will. And so to challenge the police is to challenge the American people who send them into the ghettos armed with the same self-generated fears that compelled the people who think they are white to flee the cities and into the Dream. The problem with the police is not that they are fascist pigs but that our country is ruled by majoritarian pigs.

I knew some of this even then, sitting in Rankin Chapel, even if I could not yet express it. So forgiving the killer of Prince Jones would have seemed irrelevant to me. The killer was the direct expression of all his country's beliefs. And raised conscious, in rejection of a Christian God, I could see no higher purpose in Prince's death. I believed, and still do, that our bodies are our selves, that my soul is the voltage conducted through neurons and nerves, and that my spirit is my flesh. Prince Jones was a one of one, and they had destroyed his body, scorched his shoulders and arms, ripped open his back, mangled lung, kidney, and liver. I sat there feeling myself a heretic, believing only in this one-shot life and the body. For the crime of destroying the body of Prince Jones, I did not believe in forgiveness. When the assembled mourners bowed their heads in prayer, I was divided from them because I believed that the void would not answer back.

Weeks wore on. Nauseating details slowly dribbled out. The officer was a known liar. A year earlier he had arrested a man on false evidence. Prosecutors had been forced to drop every case in which the officer was involved. The officer was demoted, restored, then put out on the street to continue his work. Now, through additional reports, a narrative began to take shape. The officer had been dressed like an undercover drug dealer. He'd been sent out to track a man whose build was five foot four and 250 pounds. We know from the coroner that Prince's body was six foot three and 211 pounds. We know that the other man was apprehended later. The charges against him were dropped. None of this mattered. We know that his superiors sent this officer to follow Prince from Maryland, through Washington, D.C., and into Virginia, where the officer shot Prince several times. We know that the officer confronted Prince with his gun drawn, and no badge. We know that the officer claims he shot because Prince tried to run him over with his jeep. We know that the authorities charged with investigating this shooting did very little to investigate the officer and did everything in their power to investigate Prince Jones. This investigation produced no information that would explain why Prince Jones would suddenly shift his ambitions from college to cop killing. This officer, given maximum power, bore minimum responsibility. He was charged with nothing. He was punished by no one. He was returned to his work.

There were times when I imagined myself, like Prince,

tracked through many jurisdictions by a man in a criminal's costume. And I was horrified, because I knew what I would have done with such a man confronting me, gun drawn, mere feet from my own family's home. *Take care of my baby,* your grandmother had said, which was to say *Take care of your new family.* But I now knew the limits of my caring, the reach of its powers, etched by an enemy old as Virginia. I thought of all the beautiful black people I'd seen at The Mecca, all their variation, all their hair, all their language, all their stories and geography, all their stunning humanity, and none of it could save them from the mark of plunder and the gravity of our particular world. And it occurred to me then that you would not escape, that there were awful men who'd laid plans for you, and I could not stop them. Prince Jones was the superlative of all my fears. And if he, good Christian, scion of a striving class, patron saint of the twice as good, could be forever bound, who then could not? And the plunder was not just of Prince alone. Think of all the love poured into him. Think of the tuitions for Montessori and music lessons. Think of the gasoline expended, the treads worn carting him to football games, basketball tournaments, and Little League. Think of the time spent regulating sleepovers. Think of the surprise birthday parties, the daycare, and the reference checks on babysitters. Think of *World Book* and *Childcraft.* Think of checks written for family photos. Think of credit cards charged for vacations. Think of soccer balls, science kits, chemistry sets, racetracks, and model trains. Think of all the embraces, all the private jokes, customs, greetings, names, dreams, all the shared knowledge and capacity of a black family injected into that vessel of flesh and bone. And think of how that vessel was taken, shattered on the concrete, and all its holy contents, all that had gone into him, sent flowing back to the earth. Think of your mother, who had no father. And your grandmother, who was abandoned by her father. And your grandfather, who was left behind by his father. And think of how Prince's daughter was now drafted into those solemn ranks and deprived of her birthright—that vessel which was her father, which brimmed with twenty-five years of love and was the investment of her grandparents and was to be her legacy.

Now at night, I held you and a great fear, wide as all our American generations, took me. Now I personally understood my father and the old mantra—"Either I can beat him or the police." I understood it all—the cable wires, the extension cords, the ritual switch. Black people love their children with a kind of obsession. You are all we have, and you come to us endangered. I think we would like to kill you ourselves before seeing you killed by the streets that America made. That is a philosophy of the disembodied, of a people who control nothing, who can protect nothing, who are made to fear not just the criminals among them but the police who lord over them with all the moral authority of a protection racket. It was only after you that I understood this love, that I understood the grip of my mother's hand. She knew that the galaxy itself could kill me, that all of me could be shattered and all of her legacy spilled upon the curb like bum wine. And no one would be brought to account for this destruction, because my death would not be the fault of any human but the fault of some unfortunate but immutable fact of "race," imposed upon an innocent country by the inscrutable judgment of invisible gods. The earthquake cannot be subpoenaed. The typhoon will not bend under indictment. They sent the killer of Prince Jones back to his work, because he was not a killer at all. He was a force of nature, the helpless agent of our world's physical laws.

This entire episode took me from fear to a rage that burned in me then, animates me now, and will likely leave me on fire for the rest of my days. I still had my journalism. My response was, in this moment, to write. I was lucky I had even that. Most of us are forced to drink our travesties straight and smile about it. I wrote about the history of the Prince George's County police. Nothing had ever felt so essential to me. Here is what I knew at the outset: The officer who killed Prince Jones was black. The politicians who empowered this officer to kill were black. Many of the black politicians, many of them twice as good, seemed unconcerned. How could this be? It was like I was back at Moorland again, called by great mysteries. But by then I didn't need any call slips; the Internet had bloomed into an instrument of research. That must strike you as novel. For all of your life, whenever you've had a question you have been able to type that question out on a keyboard, watch it appear in a rectangular space bordered by a corporate logo, and within seconds revel in the flood of potential answers. But I still remember when typewriters were useful, the dawn of the Commodore 64, and days when a song you loved would have its moment on the radio and then disappear into the nothing. I must have gone five years without hearing the Mary Jane Girls sing "All Night Long." For a young man like me, the invention of the Internet was the invention of space travel.

My curiosity, in the case of Prince Jones, opened a world of newspaper clippings, histories, and sociologies. I called politicians and questioned them. I was told that the citizens were more likely to ask for police support than to complain about brutality. I was told that the black citizens of PG County were comfortable and had "a certain impatience" with crime. I had seen these theories before, back when I was researching in Moorland, leafing through the various fights within and without the black community. I knew that these were theories, even in the mouths of black people, that justified the jails springing up around me, that argued for ghettos and projects, that viewed the destruction of the black body as incidental to the preservation of order. According to this theory "safety" was a higher value than justice, perhaps the highest value. I understood. What I would not have given, back in Baltimore, for a line of officers, agents of my country and my community, patrolling my route to school! There were no such officers, and whenever I saw the police it meant that something had already gone wrong. All along I knew that there were some, those who lived in the Dream, for whom the conversation was different. Their "safety" was in schools, portfolios, and skyscrapers. Ours was in men with guns who could only view us with the same contempt as the society that sent them.

And the lack of safety cannot help but constrain your sense of the galaxy. It never occurred to me, for instance, that I could, or should even want to, live in New York. I did love Baltimore. I loved Charlie Rudo's and the sidewalk sales at Mondawmin. I loved sitting out on the porch with your uncle Damani waiting for Frank Ski to play "Fresh Is the Word." I always thought I was destined to go back home after college—but not simply because I loved home but because I could not imagine much else for myself. And that stunted imagination is something I owe to my chains. And yet some of us really do see more.

I met many of them at The Mecca—like your uncle Ben, who was raised in New York, which forced him to understand himself as an African American navigating among Haitians, Jamaicans, Hasidic Jews, and Italians. And there were others like him, others who, having gotten a boost from a teacher, an aunt, an older brother, had peered over the wall as children, and as adults became set on seeing the full view. These black people felt, as did I, that their bodies could be snatched back at a whim, but this set in them a different kind of fear that propelled them out into the cosmos. They spent semesters abroad. I never knew what they did or why. But perhaps I always sensed I was going down too easy. Perhaps that explains every girl I've ever loved, because every girl I've ever loved was a bridge to somewhere else. Your mother, who knew so much more of the world than me, fell in love with New York through culture, through *Crossing Delancey, Breakfast at Tiffany's, Working Girl,* Nas, and Wu-Tang. Your mother secured a job, and I followed, stowed away almost, because no one in New York, at that time, was paying for me to write much of anything. What little I did make, reviewing an album or a book, covered approximately two electric bills every year.

We arrived two months before September 11, 2001. I suppose everyone who was in New York that day has a story. Here is mine: That evening, I stood on the roof of an apartment building with your mother, your aunt Chana, and her boyfriend, Jamal. So we were there on the roof, talking and taking in the sight—great plumes of smoke covered Manhattan Island. Everyone knew someone who knew someone who was missing. But looking out upon the ruins of America, my heart was cold. I had disasters all my own. The officer who killed Prince Jones, like all the officers who regard us so warily, was the sword of the American citizenry. I would never consider any American citizen pure. I was out of sync with the city. I kept thinking about how southern Manhattan had always been Ground Zero for us. They auctioned our bodies down there, in that same devastated, and rightly named, financial district. And there was once a burial ground for the auctioned there. They built a department store over part of it and then tried to erect a government building over another part. Only a community of right-thinking black people stopped them. I had not formed any of this into a coherent theory. But I did know that Bin Laden was not the first man to bring terror to that section of the city. I never forgot that. Neither should you. In the days after, I watched the ridiculous pageantry of flags, the machismo of firemen, the overwrought slogans. Damn it all. Prince Jones was dead. And hell upon those who tell us to be twice as good and shoot us no matter. Hell for ancestral fear that put black parents under terror. And hell upon those who shatter the holy vessel.

I could see no difference between the officer who killed Prince Jones and the police who died, or the firefighters who died. They were not human to me. Black, white, or whatever, they were the menaces of nature; they were the fire, the comet, the storm, which could—with no justification—shatter my body.

I saw Prince Jones, one last time, alive and whole. He was standing in front of me. We were in a museum. I felt in that moment that his death had just been an awful dream. No, a premonition. But I had a chance. I would warn him. I walked over, gave him a pound, and felt that heat of the spectrum, the warmth of The Mecca. I wanted to tell him something. I wanted to say—Beware the plunderer. But when I opened my mouth, he just shook his head and walked away.

We lived in a basement apartment in Brooklyn, which I doubt you remember, down the street from Uncle Ben and his wife, your aunt Janai. These were not great times. I remember borrowing two hundred dollars from Ben, and it feeling like a million. I remember your grandfather coming to New York, taking me out for Ethiopian, after which I walked him to the West Fourth Street subway station. We said our goodbyes and walked away. He called me back. He had forgotten something. He handed me a check for $120. I tell you this because you must understand, no matter the point of our talk, that I didn't always have things, but I had people—*I always had people.* I had a mother and father who I would match against any other. I had a brother who looked out for me all through college. I had The Mecca that directed me. I had friends who would leap in front of a bus for me. You need to know that I was loved, that whatever my lack of religious feeling, I have always loved my people and that broad love is directly related to the specific love I feel for you. I remember sitting out on Ben's stoop on Friday nights, drinking Jack Daniel's, debating the mayor's race or the rush to war. My weeks felt aimless. I pitched to various magazines with no success. Your aunt Chana lent me another two hundred dollars; I burned it all on a scam bartending school. I delivered food for a small deli in Park Slope. In New York, everyone wanted to know your occupation. I told people that I was "trying to be a writer."

Some days I would take the train into Manhattan. There was so much money everywhere, money flowing out of bistros and cafés, money pushing the people, at incredible speeds, up the wide avenues, money drawing intergalactic traffic through Times Square, money in the limestones and brownstones, money out on West Broadway where white people spilled out of wine bars with sloshing glasses and without police. I would see these people at the club, drunken, laughing, challenging breakdancers to battles. They would be destroyed and humiliated in these battles. But afterward they would give dap, laugh, order more beers. They were utterly fearless. I did not understand it until I looked out on the street. That was where I saw white parents pushing double-wide strollers down gentrifying Harlem boulevards in T-shirts and jogging shorts. Or I saw them lost in conversation with each other, mother and father, while their sons commanded entire sidewalks with their tricycles. The galaxy belonged to them, and as terror was communicated to our children, I saw mastery communicated to theirs.

And so when I remember pushing you in your stroller to other parts of the city, the West Village for instance, almost instinctively believing that you should see more, I remember feeling ill at ease, like I had borrowed someone else's heirloom, like I was traveling under an assumed name. All this time you were growing into words and feelings; my beautiful brown boy, who would soon come into the knowledge, who would soon comprehend the edicts of his galaxy, and all the extinction-level events that regarded you with a singular and discriminating interest.

You would be a man one day, and I could not save you from the unbridgeable distance between you and your future peers and colleagues, who might try to convince you that everything I know, all the things I'm sharing with you here, are an illusion, or a fact of a distant past that need not be discussed. And I could not save you from the police, from their flashlights, their hands, their nightsticks, their guns. Prince Jones, murdered by the men who should have been his security guards, is always with me, and I knew that soon he would be with you.

In those days I would come out of the house, turn onto Flatbush Avenue, and my face would tighten like a Mexican wrestler's mask, my eyes would dart from corner to corner, my arms loose, limber, and ready. This need to be always on guard was an unmeasured expenditure of energy, the slow siphoning of the essence. It contributed to the fast breakdown of our bodies. So I feared not just the violence of this world but the rules designed to protect you from it, the rules that would have you contort your body to address the block, and contort again to be taken seriously by colleagues, and contort again so as not to give the police a reason. All my life I'd heard people tell their black boys and black girls to "be twice as good," which is to say "accept half as much." These words would be spoken with a veneer of religious nobility, as though they evidenced some unspoken quality, some undetected courage, when in fact all they evidenced was the gun to our head and the hand in our pocket. This is how we lose our softness. This is how they steal our right to smile. No one told those little white children, with their tricycles, to be twice as good. I imagined their parents telling them to take twice as much. It seemed to me that our own rules redoubled plunder. It struck me that perhaps the defining feature of being drafted into the black race was the inescapable robbery of time, because the moments we spent readying the mask, or readying ourselves to accept half as much, could not be recovered. The robbery of time is not measured in lifespans but in moments. It is the last bottle of wine that you have just uncorked but do not have time to drink. It is the kiss that you do not have time to share, before she walks out of your life. It is the raft of second chances for them, and twenty-three-hour days for us.

One afternoon your mother and I took you to visit a pre-school. Our host took us down to a large gym filled with a bubbling ethnic stew of New York children. The children were running, jumping, and tumbling. You took one look at them, tore away from us, and ran right into the scrum. You have never been afraid of people, of rejection, and I have always admired you for this and always been afraid for you because of this. I watched you leap and laugh with these children you barely knew, and the wall rose in me and I felt I should grab you by the arm, pull you back and say, "We don't know these folks! Be cool!" I did not do this. I was growing, and if I could not name my anguish precisely I still knew that there was nothing noble in it. But now I understand the gravity of what I was proposing— that a four-year-old child be watchful, prudent, and shrewd, that I curtail your happiness, that you submit to a loss of time. And now when I measure this fear against the boldness that the masters of the galaxy imparted to their own children, I am ashamed.

New York was another spectrum unto itself, and the great diversity I'd seen at Howard, solely among black people, now spread across a metropolis. Something different awaited around every corner. Here there were African drummers assembling in Union Square. Here there were dead office towers, brought to life at night by restaurants buried within that served small kegs of beer and Korean fried chicken. Here there were black girls with white boys, and black boys with Chinese-American girls, and Chinese-American girls with Dominican boys, and Dominican boys with Jamaican boys and every other imaginable combination. I would walk through the West Village, marveling at restaurants the size of living rooms, and I could see that the very smallness of these restaurants awarded the patrons a kind of erudite cool, as though they were laughing at a joke, and it would take the rest of the world a decade to catch on. Summer was unreal—whole swaths of the city became fashion shows, and the avenues were nothing but runways for the youth. There was a heat unlike anything I'd ever felt, a heat from the great buildings, compounded by the millions of people jamming themselves into subway cars, into bars, into those same tiny eateries and cafés. I had never seen so much life. And I had never imagined that such life could exist in so much variety. It was everyone's particular Mecca, packed into one singular city.

But when I got off the train and came back to my hood, to my Flatbush Avenue, or my Harlem, the fear still held. It was the same boys, with the same bop, the same ice grill, and the same code I'd known all my life. If there was one difference in New York it was that we had more high-yellow cousins here in the Puerto Ricans and Dominicans. But their rituals were so similar, the way they walked and gave dap, it was all familiar to me. And so I found myself, on any given day, traveling through several New Yorks at once—dynamic, brutal, moneyed, sometimes all of those at once.

Perhaps you remember that time we went to see *Howl's Moving Castle* on the Upper West Side. You were almost five years old. The theater was crowded, and when we came out we rode a set of escalators down to the ground floor. As we came off, you were moving at the dawdling speed of a small child. A white woman pushed you and said, "Come on!" Many things now happened at once. There was the reaction of any parent when a stranger lays a hand on the body of his or her child. And there was my own insecurity in my ability to protect your black body. And more: There was my sense that this woman was pulling rank. I knew, for instance, that she would not have pushed a black child out on my part of Flatbush, because she would be afraid there and would sense, if not know, that there would be a penalty for such an action. But I was not out on my part of Flatbush. And I was not in West Baltimore. And I was far from The Mecca. I forgot all of that. I was only aware that someone had invoked their right over the body of my son. I turned and spoke to this woman, and my words were hot with all of the moment and all of my history. She shrunk back, shocked. A white man standing nearby spoke up in her defense. I experienced this as his attempt to rescue the damsel from the beast. He had made no such attempt on behalf of my son. And he was now supported by other white people in the assembling crowd. The man came closer. He grew louder. I pushed him away. He said, "I could have you arrested!" I did not care. I told him this, and the desire to do much more was hot in my throat. This desire was only controllable because I remembered someone standing off to the side there, bearing witness to more fury than he had ever seen from me—you.

I came home shook. It was a mix of shame for having gone back to the law of the streets mixed with rage—"I could have you arrested!" Which is to say: "I could take your body."

I have told this story many times, not out of bravado, but out of a need for absolution. I have never been a violent person. Even when I was young and adopted the rules of the street, anyone who knew me knew it was a bad fit. I've never felt the pride that is supposed to come with righteous self-defense and justified violence. Whenever it was me on top of someone, whatever my rage in the moment, afterward I always felt sick at having been lowered to the crudest form of communication. Malcolm made sense to me not out of a love of violence but because nothing in my life prepared me to understand tear gas as deliverance, as those Black History Month martyrs of the Civil Rights Movement did. But more than any shame I feel about my own actual violence, my greatest regret was that in seeking to defend you I was, in fact, endangering you.

"I could have you arrested," he said. Which is to say, "One of your son's earliest memories will be watching the men who sodomized Abner Louima and choked Anthony Baez cuff, club, tase, and break you." I had forgotten the rules, an error as dangerous on the Upper West Side of Manhattan as on the Westside of Baltimore. One must be without error out here. Walk in single file. Work quietly. Pack an extra number 2 pencil. Make no mistakes.

But you are human and you will make mistakes. You will misjudge. You will yell. You will drink too much. You will hang out with people you shouldn't. Not all of us can always be Jackie Robinson—not even Jackie Robinson was always Jackie Robinson. But the price of error is higher for you than it is for your countrymen, and so that America might justify itself, the story of a black body's destruction must always begin with his or her error, real or imagined—with Eric Garner's anger, with Trayvon Martin's mythical words ("You are gonna die tonight"), with Sean Bell's mistake of running with the wrong crowd, with me standing too close to the small-eyed boy pulling out.

A society, almost necessarily, begins every success story with the chapter that most advantages itself, and in America, these precipitating chapters are almost always rendered as the singular action of exceptional individuals. "It only takes one person to make a change," you are often told. This is also a myth. Perhaps one person can make a change, but not the kind of change that would raise your body to equality with your countrymen.

The fact of history is that black people have not—probably no people have ever—liberated themselves strictly through their own efforts. In every great change in the lives of African Americans we see the hand of events that were beyond our individual control, events that were not unalloyed goods. You cannot disconnect our emancipation in the Northern colonies from the blood spilled in the Revolutionary War, any more than you can disconnect our emancipation from slavery in the South from the charnel houses of the Civil War, any more than you can disconnect our emancipation from Jim Crow from the genocides of the Second World War. History is not solely in our hands. And still you are called to struggle, not because it assures you victory but because it assures you an honorable and sane life. I am ashamed of how I acted that day, ashamed of endangering your body. But I am not ashamed because I am a bad father, a bad individual or ill mannered. I am ashamed that I made an error, knowing that our errors always cost us more.

This is the import of the history all around us, though very few people like to think about it. Had I informed this woman that when she pushed my son, she was acting according to a tradition that held black bodies as lesser, her response would likely have been, "I am not a racist." Or maybe not. But my experience in this world has been that the people who believe themselves to be white are obsessed with the politics of personal exoneration. And the word *racist,* to them, conjures, if not a tobacco-spitting oaf, then something just as fantastic—an orc, troll, or gorgon. "I'm not a racist," an entertainer once insisted after being filmed repeatedly yelling at a heckler: "He's a nigger! He's a nigger!" Considering segregationist senator Strom Thurmond, Richard Nixon concluded, "Strom is no racist." There are no racists in America, or at least none that the people who need to be white know personally. In the era of mass lynching, it was so difficult to find who, specifically, served as executioner that such deaths were often reported by the press as having happened "at the hands of persons unknown." In 1957, the white residents of Levit-town, Pennsylvania, argued for their right to keep their town segregated. "As moral, religious and law-abiding cit-izens," the group wrote, "we feel that we are unprejudiced and undiscriminating in our wish to keep our community a closed community." This was the attempt to commit a shameful act while escaping all sanction, and I raise it to show you that there was no golden era when evildoers did their business and loudly proclaimed it as such.

"We would prefer to say that such people cannot exist, that there aren't any," writes Solzhenitsyn. "To do evil a human being must first of all believe that what he's doing is good, or else that it's a well-considered act in conformity with natural law." This is the foundation of the Dream—its adherents must not just believe in it but believe that it is just, believe that their possession of the Dream is the natural result of grit, honor, and good works. There is some passing acknowledgment of the bad old days, which, by the way, were not so bad as to have any ongoing effect on our present. The mettle that it takes to look away from the horror of our prison system, from police forces trans-formed into armies, from the long war against the black body, is not forged overnight. This is the practiced habit of jabbing out one's eyes and forgetting the work of one's hands. To acknowledge these horrors means turning away from the brightly rendered version of your country as it has always declared itself and turning toward something murkier and unknown. It is still too difficult for most

Americans to do this. But that is your work. It must be, if only to preserve the sanctity of your mind.

The entire narrative of this country argues against the truth of who you are. I think of that summer that you may well remember when I loaded you and your cousin Christopher into the back seat of a rented car and pushed out to see what remained of Petersburg, Shirley Plantation, and the Wilderness. I was obsessed with the Civil War because six hundred thousand people had died in it. And yet it had been glossed over in my education, and in popular culture, representations of the war and its reasons seemed obscured. And yet I knew that in 1859 we were enslaved and in 1865 we were not, and what happened to us in those years struck me as having some amount of import. But whenever I visited any of the battlefields, I felt like I was greeted as if I were a nosy accountant conducting an audit and someone was trying to hide the books.

I don't know if you remember how the film we saw at the Petersburg Battlefield ended as though the fall of the Confederacy were the onset of a tragedy, not jubilee. I doubt you remember the man on our tour dressed in the gray wool of the Confederacy, or how every visitor seemed most interested in flanking maneuvers, hardtack, smoothbore rifles, grapeshot, and ironclads, but virtually no one was interested in what all of this engineering, invention, and design had been marshaled to achieve. You were only

ten years old. But even then I knew that I must trouble you, and this meant taking you into rooms where people would insult your intelligence, where thieves would try to enlist you in your own robbery and disguise their burning and looting as Christian charity. But robbery is what this is, what it always was.

At the onset of the Civil War, our stolen bodies were worth four billion dollars, more than all of American industry, all of American railroads, workshops, and factories combined, and the prime product rendered by our stolen bodies—cotton—was America's primary export. The richest men in America lived in the Mississippi River Valley, and they made their riches off our stolen bodies. Our bodies were held in bondage by the early presidents. Our bodies were traded from the White House by James K. Polk. Our bodies built the Capitol and the National Mall. The first shot of the Civil War was fired in South Carolina, where our bodies constituted the majority of human bodies in the state. Here is the motive for the great war. It's not a secret. But we can do better and find the bandit confessing his crime. "Our position is thoroughly identified with the institution of slavery," declared Mississippi as it left the Union, "the greatest material interest of the world."

Do you remember standing with me and your mother, during one of our visits to Gettysburg, outside the home of Abraham Brian? We were with a young man who'd educated himself on the history of black people in Gettysburg. He explained that Brian Farm was the far end of the line that was charged by George Pickett on the final day of Gettysburg. He told us that Brian was a black man, that Gettysburg was home to a free black community, that Brian and his family fled their home for fear of losing their bodies to the advancing army of enslavement, led by the honored and holy Confederate general Robert E. Lee, whose army was then stealing black people from themselves and selling them south. George Pickett and his troops were repulsed by the Union Army. Standing there, a century and a half later, I thought of one of Faulkner's characters famously recalling how this failure tantalized the minds of all "Southern" boys—"It's all in the balance, it hasn't happened yet, it hasn't even begun. . . ." All of Faulkner's Southern boys were white. But I, standing on the farm of a black man who fled with his family to stay free of the South, saw Pickett's soldiers charging through history, in wild pursuit of their strange birthright—the right to beat, rape, rob, and pillage the black body. That is all of what was "in the balance," the nostalgic moment's corrupt and unspeakable core.

But American reunion was built on a comfortable narrative that made enslavement into benevolence, white knights of body snatchers, and the mass slaughter of the war into a kind of sport in which one could conclude that both sides conducted their affairs with courage, honor, and élan. This lie of the Civil War is the lie of innocence, is the Dream. Historians conjured the Dream. Hollywood fortified the Dream. The Dream was gilded by novels and adventure stories. John Carter flees the broken Confederacy for Mars. We are not supposed to ask what, precisely, he was running from. I, like every kid I knew, loved *The Dukes of Hazzard*. But I would have done well to think more about why two outlaws, driving a car named the General Lee, must necessarily be portrayed as "just some good ole boys, never meanin' no harm"—a mantra for the Dreamers if there ever was one. But what one "means" is neither important nor relevant. It is not necessary that you believe that the officer who choked Eric Garner set out that day to destroy a body. All you need to understand is that the officer carries with him the power of the American state and the weight of an American legacy, and they necessitate that of the bodies destroyed every year, some wild and disproportionate number of them will be black.

Here is what I would like for you to know: In America, it is traditional to destroy the black body—*it is heritage*. Enslavement was not merely the antiseptic borrowing of labor—it is not so easy to get a human being to commit their body against its own elemental interest. And so enslavement must be casual wrath and random manglings, the gashing of heads and brains blown out over the river as the body seeks to escape. It must be rape so regular as to be industrial. There is no uplifting way to say this. I have no praise anthems, nor old Negro spirituals. The spirit and soul are the body and brain, which are destructible—that is precisely why they are so precious. And the soul did not escape. The spirit did not steal away on gospel wings. The soul was the body that fed the tobacco, and the spirit was the blood that watered the cotton, and these created the first fruits of the American garden. And the fruits were secured through the bashing of children with stovewood, through hot iron peeling skin away like husk from corn.

It had to be blood. It had to be nails driven through tongue and ears pruned away. "Some disobedience," wrote a Southern mistress. "Much idleness, sullenness, slovenliness. . . . Used the rod." It had to be the thrashing of kitchen hands for the crime of churning butter at a leisurely clip. It had to be some woman "chear'd . . . with thirty lashes a Saturday last and as many more a Tuesday again." It could only be the employment of carriage whips, tongs, iron pokers, handsaws, stones, paperweights, or whatever might be handy to break the black body, the black family, the black community, the black nation. The bodies were pulverized into stock and marked with insurance. And the bodies were an aspiration, lucrative as Indian land, a veranda, a beautiful wife, or a summer home in the mountains. For the men who needed to believe themselves white, the bodies were the key to a social club, and the right to break the bodies was the mark of civilization. "The two great divisions of society are not the rich and poor, but white and black," said the great South Carolina senator John C. Calhoun. "And all the former, the poor as well as the rich, belong to the upper class, and are respected and treated as equals." And there it is—the right to break the black body as the meaning of their sacred equality. And that right has always given them meaning, has always meant that there was someone down in the valley because a mountain is not a mountain if there is nothing below.*

You and I, my son, are that "below." That was true in 1776. It is true today. There is no them without you, and without the right to break you they must necessarily fall from the mountain, lose their divinity, and tumble out of the Dream. And then they would have to determine how to build their suburbs on something other than human bones, how to angle their jails toward something other than a human stockyard, how to erect a democracy independent of cannibalism. But because they believe themselves to be white, they would rather countenance a man choked to death on film under their laws. And they would rather subscribe to the myth of Trayvon Martin, slight teenager, hands full of candy and soft drinks, transforming into a murderous juggernaut. And they would rather see Prince Jones followed by a bad cop through three jurisdictions and shot down for acting like a human. And they would rather reach out, in all their sanity, and push my four-year-old son as though he were merely an obstacle in the path of their too-important day.

I was there, Samori. No. I was back in Baltimore surrounded by them boys. I was on my parents' living room floor, staring out at that distant world, impenetrable to me. I was in all the anger of my years. I was where Eric Garner

---

* Thavolia Glymph, *Out of the House of Bondage.*

must have been in his last moments—"This stops today," he said and was killed. I felt the cosmic injustice, even though I did not fully understand it. I had not yet been to Gettysburg. I had not read Thavolia Glymph. All I had was the feeling, the weight. I did not yet know, and I do not fully know now. But part of what I know is that there is the burden of living among Dreamers, and there is the extra burden of your country telling you the Dream is just, noble, and real, and you are crazy for seeing the corruption and smelling the sulfur. For their innocence, they nullify your anger, your fear, until you are coming and going, and you find yourself inveighing against yourself—"Black people are the only people who . . ."—really inveighing against your own humanity and raging against the crime in your ghetto, because you are powerless before the great crime of history that brought the ghettos to be.

It is truly horrible to understand yourself as the essential below of your country. It breaks too much of what we would like to think about ourselves, our lives, the world we move through and the people who surround us. The struggle to understand is our only advantage over this madness. By the time I visited those battlefields, I knew that they had been retrofitted as the staging ground for a great deception, and this was my only security, because they could no longer insult me by lying to me. I knew—and the most important thing I knew was that, somewhere deep with them, they knew too. I like to think that knowing might have kept me from endangering you, that having understood and acknowledged the anger, I could control it. I like to think that it could have allowed me to speak the needed words to the woman and then walk away. I like to think this, but I can't promise it. The struggle is really all I have for you because it is the only portion of this world under your control.

I am sorry that I cannot make it okay. I am sorry that I cannot save you—but not that sorry. Part of me thinks that your very vulnerability brings you closer to the meaning of life, just as for others, the quest to believe oneself white divides them from it. The fact is that despite their dreams, their lives are also not inviolable. When their own vulnerability becomes real—when the police decide that tactics intended for the ghetto should enjoy wider usage, when their armed society shoots down their children, when nature sends hurricanes against their cities—they are shocked in a way that those of us who were born and bred to understand cause and effect can never be. And I would not have you live like them. You have been cast into a race in which the wind is always at your face and the hounds are always at your heels. And to varying degrees this is true of all life. The difference is that you do not have the privilege of living in ignorance of this essential fact.

I am speaking to you as I always have—as the sober and serious man I have always wanted you to be, who does not apologize for his human feelings, who does not make excuses for his height, his long arms, his beautiful smile. You are growing into consciousness, and my wish for you is that you feel no need to constrict yourself to make other people comfortable. None of that can change the math anyway. I never wanted you to be twice as good as them, so much as I have always wanted you to attack every day of your brief bright life in struggle. The people who must believe they are white can never be your measuring stick. I would not have you descend into your own dream. I would have you be a conscious citizen of this terrible and beautiful world.

One day, I was in Chicago, reporting a story about the history of segregation in the urban North and how it was engineered by government policy. I was trailing some officers of the county sheriff as they made their rounds. That day I saw a black man losing his home. I followed the sheriff's officers inside the house, where a group of them were talking to the man's wife, who was also trying to tend to her two children. She had clearly not been warned that the sheriff would be coming, though something in her husband's demeanor told me he must have known. His wife's eyes registered, all at once, shock at the circumstance, anger at the officers, and anger at her husband. The officers stood in the man's living room, giving him orders as to what would now happen. Outside there were men who'd been hired to remove the family's possessions. The man was humiliated, and I imagined that he had probably for some time carried, in his head, alone, all that was threatening his family but could not bring himself to admit it to himself or his wife. So he now changed all that energy into anger, directed at the officers. He cursed. He yelled. He pointed wildly. This particular sheriff's department was more progressive than most. They were concerned about mass incarceration. They would often bring a social worker to an eviction. But this had nothing to do with the underlying and relentless logic of the world this man inhabited, a logic built on laws built on history built on contempt for this man and his family and their fate.

The man ranted on. When the officers turned away, he ranted more to the group of black men assembled who'd been hired to sit his family out on the street. His manner was like all the powerless black people I'd ever known, exaggerating their bodies to conceal a fundamental plunder that they could not prevent.

I had spent the week exploring this city, walking through its vacant lots, watching the aimless boys, sitting in the pews of the striving churches, reeling before the street murals to the dead. And I would, from time to time, sit in the humble homes of black people in that city who were entering their tenth decade of life. These people were profound. Their homes were filled with the emblems of honorable life—citizenship awards, portraits of husbands and wives passed away, several generations of children in cap and gown. And they had drawn these accolades by cleaning big houses and living in one-room Alabama shacks before moving to the city. And they had done this

despite the city, which was supposed to be a respite, reveal-
ing itself to simply be a more intricate specimen of plunder. They had worked two and three jobs, put children
through high school and college, and become pillars of
their community. I admired them, but I knew the whole
time that I was merely encountering the survivors, the
ones who'd endured the banks and their stone-faced contempt, the realtors and their fake sympathy—"I'm sorry,
that house just sold yesterday"—the realtors who steered
them back toward ghetto blocks, or blocks earmarked to
be ghettos soon, the lenders who found this captive class
and tried to strip them of everything they had. In those
homes I saw the best of us, but behind each of them I
knew that there were so many millions gone.

And I knew that there were children born into these
same caged neighborhoods on the Westside, these ghettos,
each of which was as planned as any subdivision. They are
an elegant act of racism, killing fields authored by federal
policies, where we are, all again, plundered of our dignity,
of our families, of our wealth, and of our lives. And there
is no difference between the killing of Prince Jones and
the murders attending these killing fields because both are
rooted in the assumed inhumanity of black people. A legacy of plunder, a network of laws and traditions, a heritage,
a Dream, murdered Prince Jones as sure as it murders black
people in North Lawndale with frightening regularity.
"Black-on-black crime" is jargon, violence to language,
which vanishes the men who engineered the covenants,

who fixed the loans, who planned the projects, who built the streets and sold red ink by the barrel. And this should not surprise us. The plunder of black life was drilled into this country in its infancy and reinforced across its history, so that plunder has become an heirloom, an intelligence, a sentience, a default setting to which, likely to the end of our days, we must invariably return.

The killing fields of Chicago, of Baltimore, of Detroit, were created by the policy of Dreamers, but their weight, their shame, rests solely upon those who are dying in them. There is a great deception in this. To yell "black-on-black crime" is to shoot a man and then shame him for bleeding. And the premise that allows for these killing fields—the reduction of the black body—is no different than the premise that allowed for the murder of Prince Jones. The Dream of acting white, of talking white, of being white, murdered Prince Jones as sure as it murders black people in Chicago with frightening regularity. Do not accept the lie. Do not drink from poison. The same hands that drew red lines around the life of Prince Jones drew red lines around the ghetto.

I did not want to raise you in fear or false memory. I did not want you forced to mask your joys and bind your eyes. What I wanted for you was to grow into consciousness. I resolved to hide nothing from you.

Do you remember when I first took you to work, when

you were thirteen? I was going to see the mother of a dead black boy. The boy had exchanged hard words with a white man and been killed, because he refused to turn down his music. The killer, having emptied his gun, drove his girlfriend to a hotel. They had drinks. They ordered a pizza. And then the next day, at his leisure, the man turned himself in. The man claimed to have seen a shotgun. He claimed to have been in fear for his life and to only have triumphed through righteous violence. "I was the victim and the victor," he asserted, much as generations of American plunderers had asserted before. No shotgun was ever found. The claim still influenced the jury, and the killer was convicted not of the boy's murder but of firing repeatedly as the boy's friends tried to retreat. Destroying the black body was permissible—but it would be better to do it efficiently.

The mother of this murdered black boy was then taking her case before journalists and writers. We met her in the lobby of her Times Square hotel. She was medium height with brown skin and hair down to her shoulders. It had not even been a week since the verdict. But she was composed and wholly self-possessed. She did not rage at the killer but wondered aloud if the rules she'd imparted had been enough. She had wanted her son to stand for what he believed and to be respectful. And he had died for believing his friends had a right to play their music loud, to be American teenagers. Still, she was left wondering. "In my mind I keep saying, 'Had he not spoke back, spoke up, would he still be here?'"

She would not forget the uniqueness of her son, his singular life. She would not forget that he had a father who loved him, who took him in while she battled cancer. She would not forget that he was the life of the party, that he always had new friends for her to shuttle around in her minivan. And she would have him live on in her work. I told her the verdict angered me. I told her that the idea that someone on that jury thought it plausible there was a gun in the car baffled the mind. She said that she was baffled too, and that I should not mistake her calm probing for the absence of anger. But God had focused her anger away from revenge and toward redemption, she said. God had spoken to her and committed her to a new activism. Then the mother of the murdered boy rose, turned to you, and said, "You exist. You matter. You have value. You have every right to wear your hoodie, to play your music as loud as you want. You have every right to be you. And no one should deter you from being you. You have to be you. And you can never be afraid to be you."

I was glad she said this. I have tried to say the same to you, and if I have not said it with the same direction and clarity, I confess that is because I am afraid. And I have no God to hold me up. And I believe that when they shatter the body they shatter everything, and I knew that all of us—Christians, Muslims, atheists—lived in this fear of this truth. Disembodiment is a kind of terrorism, and the threat of it alters the orbit of all our lives and, like terrorism, this distortion is intentional. Disembodiment. The dragon that compelled the boys I knew, way back, into extravagant theater of ownership. Disembodiment. The demon that pushed the middle-class black survivors into aggressive passivity, our conversation restrained in public quarters, our best manners on display, our hands never out of pockets, our whole manner ordered as if to say, "I make no sudden moves." Disembodiment. The serpent of school years, demanding I be twice as good, though I was but a boy. Murder was all around us and we knew, deep in ourselves, in some silent space, that the author of these murders was beyond us, that it suited some other person's ends. We were right.

Here is how I take the measure of my progress in life: I imagine myself as I was, back there in West Baltimore, dodging North and Pulaski, ducking Murphy Homes, fearful of the schools and the streets, and I imagine showing that lost boy a portrait of my present life and asking him what he would make of it. Only once—in the two years after your birth, in the first two rounds of the fight of my life—have I believed he would have been disappointed. I write you at the precipice of my fortieth year, having come to a point in my life—not of great prominence—but far beyond anything that boy could have even imagined. I did not master the streets, because I could not read the body language quick enough. I did not master the schools, because I could not see where any of it could possibly lead. But I did not fall. I have my family. I have my work. I no longer feel it necessary to hang my head at parties and tell people that I am "trying to be a writer." And godless though I am, the fact of being human, the fact of possessing the gift of study, and thus being remarkable among all the matter floating through the cosmos, still awes me.

I have spent much of my studies searching for the right question by which I might fully understand the breach between the world and me. I have not spent my time studying the problem of "race"—"race" itself is just a restatement and retrenchment of the problem. You see this from time to time when some dullard—usually believing himself white—proposes that the way forward is a grand orgy of black and white, ending only when we are all beige and thus the same "race." But a great number of "black" people already are beige. And the history of civilization is littered with dead "races" (Frankish, Italian, German, Irish) later abandoned because they no longer serve their purpose—the organization of people beneath, and beyond, the umbrella of rights.

If my life ended today, I would tell you it was a happy life—that I drew great joy from the study, from the struggle toward which I now urge you. You have seen in this conversation that the struggle has ruptured and remade me several times over—in Baltimore, at The Mecca, in father-hood, in New York. The changes have awarded me a rap-ture that comes only when you can no longer be lied to, when you have rejected the Dream. But even more, the changes have taught me how to best exploit that singular gift of study, to question what I see, then to question what I see after that, because the questions matter as much, per-haps more than, the answers.

But oh, my eyes. When I was a boy, no portion of my body suffered more than my eyes. If I have done well by the measures of childhood, it must be added that those measures themselves are hampered by how little a boy of my captive class had seen. The Dream seemed to be the pinnacle, then—to grow rich and live in one of those dis-connected houses out in the country, in one of those small communities, one of those cul-de-sacs with its gently curving ways, where they staged teen movies and children built treehouses, and in that last lost year before college, teenagers made love in cars parked at the lake. The Dream seemed to be the end of the world for me, the height of American ambition. What more could possibly exist be-yond the dispatches, beyond the suburbs?

Your mother knew. Perhaps it was because she was raised within the physical borders of such a place, because she lived in proximity with the Dreamers. Perhaps it was because the people who thought they were white told her she was smart and followed this up by telling her she was not really black, meaning it as a compliment. Perhaps it

was the boys out there, who were in fact black, telling her she was "pretty for a dark-skin girl." Your mother never felt quite at home, and this made the possibility of some other place essential to her, propelling her to The Mecca, propelling her to New York and then beyond. On her thirtieth birthday she took a trip to Paris. I am not sure you remember. You were only six. We spent that week eating fried fish for breakfast and cake for dinner, leaving underwear on the counter, and blasting Ghostface Killah. It had never occurred to me to leave America—not even temporarily. My eyes. My friend Jelani, who came up the same as me, once said that he used to think of traveling as a pointless luxury, like blowing the rent check on a pink suit. And I felt much the same, then. I was bemused at your mother's dreams of Paris. I could not understand them—and I did not think I needed to. Some part of me was still back in that seventh-grade French class, thinking only of the immediate security of my body, regarding France as one might regard Jupiter.

But now your mother had gone and done it, and when she returned her eyes were dancing with all the possibilities out there, not just for her but for you and for me. It is quite ridiculous how the feeling spread. It was like falling in love—the things that get you are so small, the things that keep you up at night are so particular to you that when you try to explain, the only reward anyone can give you is a dumb polite nod. Your mother had taken many pictures, all through Paris, of doors, giant doors—deep

blue, ebony, orange, turquoise, and burning red doors. I examined the pictures of these giant doors in our small Harlem apartment. I had never seen anything like them. It had never even occurred to me that such giant doors could exist, could be so common in one part of the world and totally absent in another. And it occurred to me, listening to your mother, that France was not a thought experiment but an actual place filled with actual people whose traditions were different, whose lives really were different, whose sense of beauty was different.

When I look back, I know that I was then getting the message from all over. By that time my friends included a great number of people with ties to different worlds. "Make the race proud," the elders used to say. But by then I knew that I wasn't so much bound to a biological "race" as to a group of people, and these people were not black because of any uniform color or any uniform physical feature. They were bound because they suffered under the weight of the Dream, and they were bound by all the beautiful things, all the language and mannerisms, all the food and music, all the literature and philosophy, all the common language that they fashioned like diamonds under the weight of the Dream. Not long ago I was standing in an airport retrieving a bag from a conveyor belt. I bumped into a young black man and said, "My bad." Without even looking up he said, "You straight." And in that exchange there was so much of the private rapport that can only exist between two particular strangers of this tribe that we call black. In other words, I was part of a world. And looking out, I had friends who too were part of other worlds—the world of Jews or New Yorkers, the world of Southerners or gay men, of immigrants, of Californians, of Native Americans, or a combination of any of these, worlds stitched into worlds like tapestry. And though I could never, myself, be a native of any of these worlds, I knew that nothing so essentialist as race stood between us. I had read too much by then. And my eyes—my beautiful, precious eyes—were growing stronger each day. And I saw that what divided me from the world was not anything intrinsic to us but the actual injury done by people intent on naming us, intent on believing that what they have named us matters more than anything we could ever actually do. In America, the injury is not in being born with darker skin, with fuller lips, with a broader nose, but in everything that happens after. In that single exchange with that young man, I was speaking the personal language of my people. It was the briefest intimacy, but it captured much of the beauty of my black world—the ease between your mother and me, the miracle at The Mecca, the way I feel myself disappear on the streets of Harlem. To call that feeling racial is to hand over all those diamonds, fashioned by our ancestors, to the plunderer. We made that feeling, though it was forged in the shadow of the murdered, the raped, the disembodied, we made it all the same. This is the beautiful thing that I have seen with my own eyes, and

I think I needed this vantage point before I could journey out. I think I needed to know that I was from somewhere, that my home was as beautiful as any other.

Seven years after I saw the pictures of those doors, I received my first adult passport. I wish I had come to it sooner. I wish, when I was back in that French class, that I had connected the conjugations, verbs, and gendered nouns to something grander. I wish someone had told me what that class really was—a gate to some other blue world. I wanted to see that world myself, to see the doors and everything behind them. The day of my departure, I sat in a restaurant with your mother, who'd shown me so much. I told her, "I am afraid." I didn't really speak the language. I did not know the customs. I would be alone. She just listened and held my hand. And that night, I boarded a starship. The starship punched out into the dark, punched through the sky, punched out past West Baltimore, punched out past The Mecca, past New York, past any language and every spectrum known to me.

My ticket took me to Geneva first. Everything happened very fast. I had to change money. I needed to find a train from the airport into the city and after that find another train to Paris. Some months earlier, I had begun a halting study of the French language. Now I was in a storm of French, drenched really, and only equipped to catch drops of the language—"who," "euros," "you," "to the right." I was still very afraid.

I surveyed the railway schedule and became aware that

I was one wrong ticket from Vienna, Milan, or some Alpine village that no one I knew had ever heard of. It happened right then. The realization of being far gone, the fear, the unknowable possibilities, all of it—the horror, the wonder, the joy—fused into an erotic thrill. The thrill was not wholly alien. It was close to the wave that came over me in Moorland. It was kin to the narcotic shot I'd gotten watching the people with their wineglasses spill out onto West Broadway. It was all that I'd felt looking at those Parisian doors. And at that moment I realized that those changes, with all their agony, awkwardness, and confusion, were the defining fact of my life, and for the first time I knew not only that I really was alive, that I really was studying and observing, but that I had long been alive—even back in Baltimore. I had always been alive. I was always translating.

I arrived in Paris. I checked in to a hotel in the 6th arrondissement. I had no understanding of the local history at all. I did not think much about Baldwin or Wright. I had not read Sartre nor Camus, and if I walked past Café de Flore or Les Deux Magots I did not, then, take any particular note. None of that mattered. It was Friday, and what mattered were the streets thronged with people in amazing configurations. Teenagers together in cafés. Schoolchildren kicking a soccer ball on the street, backpacks to the side. Older couples in long coats, billowing scarves, and blazers. Twentysomethings leaning out of any number of establishments looking beautiful and cool. It recalled New York, but without the low-grade, ever-present fear. The people wore no armor, or none that I recognized. Side streets and alleys were bursting with bars, restaurants, and cafés. Everyone was walking. Those who were not walking were embracing. I was feeling myself beyond any natural right. My Caesar was geometric. My lineup was sharp as a sword. I walked outside and melted into the city, like butter in the stew. In my mind, I heard Big Boi sing:

*I'm just a playa like that, my jeans was sharply creased.*
*I got a fresh white T-shirt and my cap is slightly pointed east.*

I had dinner with a friend. The restaurant was the size of two large living rooms. The tables were jammed together, and to be seated, the waitress employed a kind of magic, pulling one table out and then wedging you in, like a child in a high chair. You had to summon her to use the toilet. When it was time to order, I flailed at her with my catastrophic French. She nodded and did not laugh. She gave no false manners. We had an incredible bottle of wine. I had steak. I had a baguette with bone marrow. I had liver. I had an espresso and a dessert that I can't even name. Using all the French I could muster, I tried to tell the waitress the meal was magnificent. She cut me off in English, "The best you've ever had, right?" I rose to walk, and despite having inhaled half the menu I felt easy as a featherweight. The next day I got up early and walked through the city. I visited the Musée Rodin. I stopped in a bistro, and with all the fear of a boy approaching a beautiful girl at a party, I ordered two beers and then a burger. I walked to Le Jardin du Luxembourg. It was about four o'clock in the afternoon. I took a seat. The garden was bursting with people, again in all their alien ways. At that moment a strange loneliness took hold. Perhaps it was that I had not spoken a single word of English that entire day. Perhaps it was that I had never sat in a public garden before, had not even known it to be something that I'd want to do. And all around me there were people who did this regularly.

It occurred to me that I really was in someone else's country and yet, in some necessary way, I was outside of their country. In America I was part of an equation—even if it wasn't a part I relished. I was the one the police stopped on Twenty-third Street in the middle of a workday. I was the one driven to The Mecca. I was not just a father but the father of a black boy. I was not just a spouse but the husband of a black woman, a freighted symbol of black love. But sitting in that garden, for the first time I was an alien, I was a sailor—landless and disconnected. And I was sorry that I had never felt this particular loneliness before— that I had never felt myself so far outside of someone else's dream. Now I felt the deeper weight of my generational chains—my body confined, by history and policy, to certain zones. Some of us make it out. But the game is played with loaded dice. I wished I had known more, and I wished

I had known it sooner. I remember, that night, watching the teenagers gathering along the pathway near the Seine to do all their teenage things. And I remember thinking how much I would have loved for that to have been my life, how much I would have loved to have a past apart from the fear. I did not have that past in hand or memory. But I had you.

We came back to Paris that summer, because your mother loved the city and because I loved the language, but above all because of you.

I wanted you to have your own life, apart from fear— even apart from me. I am wounded. I am marked by old codes, which shielded me in one world and then chained me in the next. I think of your grandmother calling me and noting how you were growing tall and would one day try to "test me." And I said to her that I would regard that day, should it come, as the total failure of fatherhood because if all I had over you were my hands, then I really had nothing at all. But, forgive me, son, I knew what she meant and when you were younger I thought the same. And I am now ashamed of the thought, ashamed of my fear, of the generational chains I tried to clasp onto your wrists. We are entering our last years together, and I wish I had been softer with you. Your mother had to teach me how to love you—how to kiss you and tell you I love you every night. Even now it does not feel a wholly natural act so much as it feels like ritual. And that is because I am wounded. That is because I am tied to old ways, which I learned in a hard house. It was a loving house even as it was besieged by its country, but it *was* hard. Even in Paris, I could not shake the old ways, the instinct to watch my back at every pass, and always be ready to go.

A few weeks into our stay, I made a friend who wanted to improve his English as much as I wanted to improve my French. We met one day out in the crowd in front of Notre Dame. We walked to the Latin Quarter. We walked to a wine shop. Outside the wine shop there was seating. We sat and drank a bottle of red. We were served heaping piles of meats, bread, and cheese. Was this dinner? Did people do this? I had not even known how to imagine it. And more, was this all some elaborate ritual to get an angle on me? My friend paid. I thanked him. But when we left I made sure he walked out first. He wanted to show me one of those old buildings that seem to be around every corner in that city. And the entire time he was leading me, I was sure he was going to make a quick turn into an alley, where some dudes would be waiting to strip me of . . . what, exactly? But my new friend simply showed me the building, shook my hand, gave a fine *bonne soirée,* and walked off into the wide open night. And watching him walk away, I felt that I had missed part of the experience because of my eyes, because my eyes were made in Baltimore, because my eyes were blindfolded by fear.

What I wanted was to put as much distance between you and that blinding fear as possible. I wanted you to see different people living by different rules. I wanted you to see the couples sitting next to each other in the cafés, turned out to watch the street; the women pedaling their old bikes up the streets, without helmets, in long white dresses; the women whizzing past in Daisy Dukes and pink roller skates. I wanted you to see the men in salmon-colored pants and white linen and bright sweaters tied around their necks, the men who disappeared around corners and circled back in luxury cars, with the top down, loving their lives. All of them smoking. All of them knowing that either grisly death or an orgy awaited them just around the corner. Do you remember how your eyes lit up like candles when we stood out on Saint-Germain-des-Prés? That look was all that I lived for.

And even then, I wanted you to be conscious, to understand that to be distanced, if only for a moment, from fear is not a passport out of the struggle. We will always be black, you and I, even if it means different things in different places. France is built on its own dream, on its collection of bodies, and recall that your very name is drawn from a man who opposed France and its national project of theft by colonization. It is true that our color was not our distinguishing feature there, so much as the American-ness represented in our poor handle on French. And it is true that there is something particular about how the Americans who think they are white regard us—something sexual and obscene. We were not enslaved in France. We are not their particular "problem," nor their national guilt. We are not their niggers. If there is any comfort in this, it is not the kind that I would encourage you to indulge. Remember your name. Remember that you and I are brothers, are the children of trans-Atlantic rape. Remember the broader consciousness that comes with that. Remember that this consciousness can never ultimately be racial; it must be cosmic. Remember the Roma you saw begging with their children in the street, and the venom with which they were addressed. Remember the Algerian cab driver, speaking openly of his hatred of Paris, then looking at your mother and me and insisting that we were all united under Africa. Remember the rumbling we all felt under the beauty of Paris, as though the city had been built in abeyance of Pompeii. Remember the feeling that the great public gardens, the long lunches, might all be undone by a physics, cousin to our rules and the reckoning of our own country, that we do not fully comprehend.

It was good to have your uncle Ben and your aunt Janai there—someone else who had to balance the awe of what these people had built and the fact of whom they built so much of it upon; someone else who'd learned to travel in adulthood; people who'd been black in America and were mostly concerned with the safety of their bodies. And we were all aware that the forces that held back our bodies back at home were not unrelated to those that had given France its wealth. We were aware that much of what they had done was built on the plunder of Haitian bodies, on the plunder of Wolof bodies, on the destruction of the Toucouleur, on the taking of Bissandugu.

That was the same summer that the killer of Trayvon Martin was acquitted, the summer I realized that I accepted that there is no velocity of escape. Home would find us in any language. Remember when we took the train up to Place de la Nation to celebrate your birthday with Janai and Ben and the kids? Remember the young man standing outside the subway in protest? Do you remember his sign? VIVE LE COMBAT DES JEUNES CONTRE LE CRIMES RACISTES! USA: TRAYVON MARTIN, 17 ANS ASSASSINÉ CAR NOIR ET LE RACISTE ACQUITTÉ.

I did not die in my aimless youth. I did not perish in the agony of not knowing. I was not jailed. I had proven to myself that there was another way beyond the schools and the streets. I felt myself to be among the survivors of some great natural disaster, some plague, some avalanche or earthquake. And now, living in the wake of a decimation and having arrived at a land that I once considered mythical, everything seemed cast in a halo—the pastel Parisian scarves burned brighter, the morning odor wafting out of the boulangeries was hypnotic, and the language all around me struck me not so much as language but as dance.

Your route will be different. It must be. You knew things at eleven that I did not know when I was twenty-five. When I was eleven my highest priority was the simple

security of my body. My life was the immediate negotia-
tion of violence—within my house and without. But already you have expectations, I see that in you. Survival and
safety are not enough. Your hopes—your dreams, if you
will—leave me with an array of warring emotions. I am so
very proud of you—your openness, your ambition, your
aggression, your intelligence. My job, in the little time we
have left together, is to match that intelligence with wisdom. Part of that wisdom is understanding what you were
given—a city where gay bars are unremarkable, a soccer
team on which half the players speak some other language.
What I am saying is that it does not all belong to you, that
the beauty in you is not strictly yours and is largely the
result of enjoying an abnormal amount of security in your
black body.

Perhaps that is why, when you discovered that the killer
of Mike Brown would go unpunished, you told me you
had to go. Perhaps that is why you were crying, because in
that moment you understood that even your relatively
privileged security can never match a sustained assault
launched in the name of the Dream. Our current politics
tell you that should you fall victim to such an assault and
lose your body, it somehow must be your fault. Trayvon
Martin's hoodie got him killed. Jordan Davis's loud music
did the same. John Crawford should never have touched
the rifle on display. Kajieme Powell should have known
not to be crazy. And all of them should have had fathers—

even the ones who had fathers, even you. Without its own justifications, the Dream would collapse upon itself. You first learned this from Michael Brown. I first learned it from Prince Jones.

Michael Brown did not die as so many of his defenders supposed. And still the questions behind the questions are never asked. Should assaulting an officer of the state be a capital offense, rendered without trial, with the officer as judge and executioner? Is that what we wish civilization to be? And all the time the Dreamers are pillaging Ferguson for municipal governance. And they are torturing Muslims, and their drones are bombing wedding parties (by accident!), and the Dreamers are quoting Martin Luther King and exulting nonviolence for the weak and the biggest guns for the strong. Each time a police officer engages us, death, injury, maiming is possible. It is not enough to say that this is true of anyone or more true of criminals. The moment the officers began their pursuit of Prince Jones, his life was in danger. The Dreamers accept this as the cost of doing business, accept our bodies as currency, because it is their tradition. As slaves we were this country's first windfall, the down payment on its freedom. After the ruin and liberation of the Civil War came Redemption for the unrepentant South and Reunion, and our bodies became this country's second mortgage. In the New Deal we were their guestroom, their finished basement. And today, with a sprawling prison system, which has turned the warehousing of black bodies into a jobs program for Dreamers and a lucrative investment for Dreamers; today, when 8 percent of the world's prisoners are black men, our bodies have refinanced the Dream of being white. Black life is cheap, but in America black bodies are a natural resource of incomparable value.

# III.

*And have brought humanity to the edge of
oblivion: because they think they are white.*

JAMES BALDWIN

In the years after Prince Jones died, I thought often of those who were left to make their lives in the shadow of his death. I thought of his fiancée and wondered what it meant to see the future upended with no explanation. I wondered what she would tell his daughter, and I wondered how his daughter would imagine her father, when she would miss him, how she would detail the loss. But mostly I wondered about Prince's mother, and the question I mostly asked myself was always the same: How did she live? I searched for her phone number online. I emailed her. She responded. Then I called and made an appointment to visit. And living she was, just outside of Philadelphia in a small gated community of affluent homes. It was a rainy Tuesday when I arrived. I had taken the train in from New York and then picked up a rental car. I was thinking of Prince a lot in those months before. You, your mother, and I had gone to Homecoming at The Mecca, and so many of my friends were there, and Prince was not.

Dr. Jones greeted me at the door. She was lovely, polite, brown. She appeared to be somewhere in that range between forty and seventy years, when it becomes difficult to precisely ascertain a black person's precise age. She was well composed, given the subject of our conversation, and for most of the visit I struggled to separate how she actually felt from what I felt she must be feeling. What I felt, right then, was that she was smiling through pained eyes, that the reason for my visit had spread sadness like a dark quilt over the whole house. I seem to recall music—jazz or gospel—playing in the back, but conflicting with that I also remember a deep quiet overcoming everything. I thought that perhaps she had been crying. I could not tell for sure. She led me into her large living room. There was no one else in the house. It was early January. Her Christmas tree was still standing at the end of the room, and there were stockings bearing the name of her daughter and her lost son, and there was a framed picture of him—Prince Jones—on a display table. She brought me water in a heavy glass. She drank tea. She told me that she was born and raised outside of Opelousas, Louisiana, that her ancestors had been enslaved in that same region, and that as a consequence of that enslavement, a fear echoed down through the ages. "It first became clear when I was four," she told me.

My mother and I were going into the city. We got on the Greyhound bus. I was behind my mother. She wasn't holding my hand at the time and I plopped down in the first seat I found. A few minutes later my mother was looking for me and she took me to the back of the bus and explained why I couldn't sit there. We were very poor, and most of the black people around us, who I knew were poor also, and the images I had of white America were from going into the city and seeing who was behind the counter in the stores and seeing who my mother worked for. It became clear there was a distance.

This chasm makes itself known to us in all kinds of ways. A little girl wanders home, at age seven, after being teased in school and asks her parents, "Are we niggers and what does this mean?" Sometimes it is subtle—the simple observation of who lives where and works what jobs and who does not. Sometimes it's all of it at once. I have never asked how you became personally aware of the distance. Was it Mike Brown? I don't think I want to know. But I know that it has happened to you already, that you have deduced that you are privileged and yet still different from other privileged children, because you are the bearer of a body more fragile than any other in this country. What I want you to know is that this is not your fault, even if it is ultimately your responsibility. It is your responsibility because you are surrounded by the Dreamers. It has nothing to do with how you wear your pants or how you style your hair. The breach is as intentional as policy, as intentional as the forgetting that follows. The breach allows for the efficient sorting of the plundered from the plunderers, the enslaved from the enslavers, sharecroppers from landholders, cannibals from food.

Dr. Jones was reserved. She was what people once referred to as "a lady," and in that sense reminded me of my grandmother, who was a single mother in the projects but always spoke as though she had nice things. And when Dr. Jones described her motive for escaping the dearth that marked the sharecropper life of her father and all the others around her, when she remembered herself saying, "I'm not going to live like this," I saw the iron in her eyes, and I remembered the iron in my grandmother's eyes. You must barely remember her by now—you were six when she died. I remember her, of course, but by the time I knew her, her exploits—how, for instance, she scrubbed white people's floors during the day and went to school at night—were legend. But I still could feel the power and rectitude that propelled her out of the projects and into homeownership.

It was the same power I felt in the presence of Dr. Jones. When she was in second grade, she and another girl made a pact that they would both become doctors, and she held up her end of the bargain. But first she integrated the high school in her town. At the beginning she fought the white children who insulted her. At the end they voted her class president. She ran track. It was "a great entrée," she told me, but it only brought her so far into their world. At football games the other students would cheer the star black running back, and then when a black player on the other team got the ball, they'd yell, "Kill that nigger! Kill that nigger!" They would yell this sitting right next to her, as though she really were not there. She gave Bible recitations as a child and told me the story of her recruitment into this business. Her mother took her to audition for the junior choir. Afterward the choir director said, "Honey, I think you should talk." She was laughing lightly now, not uproariously, still in control of her body. I felt that she was warming up. As she talked of the church, I thought of your grandfather, the one you know, and how his first intellectual adventures were found in the recitation of Bible passages. I thought of your mother, who did the same. And I thought of my own distance from an institution that has, so often, been the only support for our people. I often wonder if in that distance I've missed something, some notions of cosmic hope, some wisdom beyond my mean physical perception of the world, something beyond the body, that I might have transmitted to you. I wondered this, at that particular moment, because something beyond anything I have ever understood drove Mable Jones to an exceptional life.

She went to college on full scholarship. She went to med school at Louisiana State University. She served in the

Navy. She took up radiology. She did not then know any other black radiologists. I assumed that this would have been hard on her, but she was insulted by the assumption. She could not acknowledge any discomfort, and she did not speak of herself as remarkable, because it conceded too much, because it sanctified tribal expectations when the only expectation that mattered should be rooted in an assessment of Mable Jones. And by those lights, there was nothing surprising in her success, because Mable Jones was always pedal to the floor, not over or around, but through, and if she was going to do it, it must be done to death. Her disposition toward life was that of an elite athlete who knows the opponent is dirty and the refs are on the take, but also knows the championship is one game away.

She called her son—Prince Jones—"Rocky" in honor of her grandfather, who went by "Rock." I asked about his childhood, because the fact is that I had not known Prince all that well. He was among the people I would be happy to see at a party, whom I would describe to a friend as "a good brother," though I could not really account for his comings and goings. So she sketched him for me so that I might better understand. She said that he once hammered a nail into an electrical socket and shorted out the entire house. She said that he once dressed himself in a suit and tie, got down on one knee, and sang "Three Times a Lady" to her. She said that he'd gone to private schools his entire life—schools filled with Dreamers—but he made friends wherever he went, in Louisiana and later in Texas. I asked her how his friends' parents treated her. "By then I was the chief of radiology at the local hospital," she said. "And so they treated me with respect." She said this with no love in her eye, coldly, as though she were explaining a mathematical function.

Like his mother, Prince was smart. In high school he was admitted to a Texas magnet school for math and science, where students acquire college credit. Despite the school drawing from a state with roughly the population of Angola, Australia, or Afghanistan, Prince was the only black child. I asked Dr. Jones if she had wanted him to go to Howard. She smiled and said, "No." Then she added, "It's so nice to be able to talk about this." This relaxed me a little, because I could think of myself as something more than an intrusion. I asked where she had wanted him to go for college. She said, "Harvard. And if not Harvard, Princeton. And if not Princeton, Yale. And if not Yale, Columbia. And if not Columbia, Stanford. He was that caliber of student." But like at least one third of all the students who came to Howard, Prince was tired of having to represent to other people. These Howard students were not like me. They were the children of the Jackie Robinson elite, whose parents rose up out of the ghettos, and the sharecropping fields, went out into the suburbs, only to find that they carried the mark with them and could not escape. Even when they succeeded, as so many of them did, they were singled out, made examples of, transfigured into parables of diversity. They were symbols and markers, never children or young adults. And so they come to Howard to be normal—and even more, to see how broad the black normal really is.

Prince did not apply to Harvard, nor Princeton, nor Yale, nor Columbia, nor Stanford. He only wanted The Mecca. I asked Dr. Jones if she regretted Prince choosing Howard. She gasped. It was as though I had pushed too hard on a bruise. "No," she said. "I regret that he is dead."

She said this with great composure and greater pain. She said this with all of the odd poise and direction that the great American injury demands of you. Have you ever taken a hard look at those pictures from the sit-ins in the '60s, a hard, serious look? Have you ever looked at the faces? The faces are neither angry, nor sad, nor joyous. They betray almost no emotion. They look out past their tormentors, past us, and focus on something way beyond anything known to me. I think they are fastened to their god, a god whom I cannot know and in whom I do not believe. But, god or not, the armor is all over them, and it is real. Or perhaps it is not armor at all. Perhaps it is life extension, a kind of loan allowing you to take the assaults heaped upon you now and pay down the debt later. Whatever it is, that same look I see in those pictures, noble and vacuous, was the look I saw in Mable Jones. It was in her sharp brown eyes, which welled but did not break. She held so much under her control, and I was sure the days since her Rocky was plundered, since her lineage was robbed, had demanded nothing less.

And she could not lean on her country for help. When it came to her son, Dr. Jones's country did what it does best—it forgot him. The forgetting is habit, is yet another necessary component of the Dream. They have forgotten the scale of theft that enriched them in slavery; the terror that allowed them, for a century, to pilfer the vote; the segregationist policy that gave them their suburbs. They have forgotten, because to remember would tumble them out of the beautiful Dream and force them to live down here with us, down here in the world. I am convinced that the Dreamers, at least the Dreamers of today, would rather live white than live free. In the Dream they are Buck Rogers, Prince Aragorn, an entire race of Skywalkers. To awaken them is to reveal that they are an empire of humans and, like all empires of humans, are built on the destruction of the body. It is to stain their nobility, to make them vulnerable, fallible, breakable humans.

Dr. Jones was asleep when the phone rang. It was 5 A.M. and on the phone was a detective telling her she should drive to Washington. Rocky was in the hospital. Rocky had been shot. She drove with her daughter. She was sure he was still alive. She paused several times as she explained this. She went directly to the ICU. Rocky was not there. A group of men with authority—doctors, lawyers, detectives, perhaps—took her into a room and told her he was gone. She paused again. She did not cry. Composure was too important now.

"It was unlike anything I had felt before," she told me. "It was extremely physically painful. So much so that whenever a thought of him would come to mind, all I could do was pray and ask for mercy. I thought I was going to lose my mind and go crazy. I felt sick. I felt like I was dying."

I asked if she expected that the police officer who had shot Prince would be charged. She said, "Yes." Her voice was a cocktail of emotions. She spoke like an American, with the same expectations of fairness, even fairness belated and begrudged, that she took into medical school all those years ago. And she spoke like a black woman, with all the pain that undercuts those exact feelings.

I now wondered about her daughter, who'd been recently married. There was a picture on display of this daughter and her new husband. Dr. Jones was not optimistic. She was intensely worried about her daughter bringing a son into America, because she could not save him, she could not secure his body from the ritual violence that had claimed her son. She compared America to Rome. She said she thought the glory days of this country had long ago passed, and even those glory days were sullied: They had been built on the bodies of others. "And we can't get the message," she said. "We don't understand that we are embracing our deaths."

I asked Dr. Jones if her mother was still alive. She told me her mother passed away in 2002, at the age of eighty-nine. I asked Dr. Jones how her mother had taken Prince's death, and her voice retreated into an almost-whisper, and Dr. Jones said, "I don't know that she did."

She alluded to *12 Years a Slave*. "There he was," she said, speaking of Solomon Northup. "He had means. He had a family. He was living like a human being. And one racist act took him back. And the same is true of me. I spent years developing a career, acquiring assets, engaging responsibilities. And one racist act. It's all it takes." And then she talked again of all that she had, through great industry, through unceasing labor, acquired in the long journey from grinding poverty. She spoke of how her children had been raised in the lap of luxury—annual ski trips, jaunts off to Europe. She said that when her daughter was studying Shakespeare in high school, she took her to England. And when her daughter got her license at sixteen, a Mazda 626 was waiting in front. I sensed some connection to this desire to give and the raw poverty of her youth. I sensed that it was all as much for her as it was for her children. She said that Prince had never taken to material things. He loved to read. He loved to travel. But when he turned twenty-three, she bought him a jeep. She had a huge purple bow put on it. She told me that she could still see him there, looking at the jeep and simply saying, *Thank you, Mom*. Without interruption she added, "And that was the jeep he was killed in."

After I left, I sat in the car, idle for a few minutes. I thought of all that Prince's mother had invested in him, and all that was lost. I thought of the loneliness that sent him to The Mecca, and how The Mecca, how we, could not save him, how we ultimately cannot save ourselves. I thought back on the sit-ins, the protestors with their stoic faces, the ones I'd once scorned for hurling their bodies at the worst things in life. Perhaps they had known something terrible about the world. Perhaps they so willingly parted with the security and sanctity of the black body because neither security nor sanctity existed in the first place. And all those old photographs from the 1960s, all those films I beheld of black people prostrate before clubs and dogs, were not simply shameful, indeed were not shameful at all—they were just true. We are captured, brother, surrounded by the majoritarian bandits of America. And this has happened here, in our only home, and the terrible truth is that we cannot will ourselves to an escape on our own. Perhaps that was, is, the hope of the movement: to awaken the Dreamers, to rouse them to the facts of what their need to be white, to talk like they are white, to think that they are white, which is to think that they are beyond the design flaws of humanity, has done to the world.

But you cannot arrange your life around them and the small chance of the Dreamers coming into consciousness. Our moment is too brief. Our bodies are too precious. And you are here now, and you must live—and there is so much out there to live for, not just in someone else's country, but in your own home. The warmth of dark energies that drew me to The Mecca, that drew out Prince Jones, the warmth of our particular world, is beautiful, no matter how brief and breakable.

I think back to our trip to Homecoming. I think back to the warm blasts rolling over us. We were at the football game. We were sitting in the bleachers with old friends and their children, caring for neither fumbles nor first downs. I remember looking toward the goalposts and watching a pack of alumni cheerleaders so enamored with Howard University that they donned their old colors and took out their old uniforms just a little so they'd fit. I remember them dancing. They'd shake, freeze, shake again, and when the crowd yelled "Do it! Do it! Do it! Dooo it!" a black woman two rows in front of me, in her tightest jeans, stood and shook as though she was not somebody's momma and the past twenty years had barely been a week. I remember walking down to the tailgate party without you. I could not bring you, but I have no problem telling you what I saw—the entire diaspora around me—hustlers, lawyers, Kappas, busters, doctors, barbers, Deltas, drunkards, geeks, and nerds. The DJ hollered into the mic. The young folks pushed toward him. A young man pulled out a bottle of cognac and twisted the cap. A girl with him smiled, tilted her head back, imbibed, laughed. And I felt myself disappearing into all of their bodies. The birthmark of damnation faded, and I could feel the weight of my arms and

hear the heave in my breath and I was not talking then, because there was no point.

That was a moment, a joyous moment, beyond the Dream—a moment imbued by a power more gorgeous than any voting rights bill. This power, this black power, originates in a view of the American galaxy taken from a dark and essential planet. Black power is the dungeon-side view of Monticello—which is to say, the view taken in struggle. And black power births a kind of understanding that illuminates all the galaxies in their truest colors. Even the Dreamers—lost in their great reverie—feel it, for it is Billie they reach for in sadness, and Mobb Deep is what they holler in boldness, and Isley they hum in love, and Dre they yell in revelry, and Aretha is the last sound they hear before dying. We have made something down here. We have taken the one-drop rules of Dreamers and flipped them. They made us into a race. We made ourselves into a people. Here at The Mecca, under pain of selection, we have made a home. As do black people on summer blocks marked with needles, vials, and hopscotch squares. As do black people dancing it out at rent parties, as do black people at their family reunions where we are regarded like the survivors of catastrophe. As do black people toasting their cognac and German beers, passing their blunts and debating MCs. As do all of us who have voyaged through death, to life upon these shores.

That was the love power that drew Prince Jones. The

power is not divinity but a deep knowledge of how fragile everything—even the Dream, especially the Dream—really is. Sitting in that car I thought of Dr. Jones's predictions of national doom. I had heard such predictions all my life from Malcolm and all his posthumous followers who hollered that the Dreamers must reap what they sow. I saw the same prediction in the words of Marcus Garvey who promised to return in a whirlwind of vengeful ancestors, an army of Middle Passage undead. No. I left The Mecca knowing that this was all too pat, knowing that should the Dreamers reap what they had sown, we would reap it right with them. Plunder has matured into habit and addiction; the people who could author the mechanized death of our ghettos, the mass rape of private prisons, then engineer their own forgetting, must inevitably plunder much more. This is not a belief in prophecy but in the seductiveness of cheap gasoline.

Once, the Dream's parameters were caged by technology and by the limits of horsepower and wind. But the Dreamers have improved themselves, and the damming of seas for voltage, the extraction of coal, the transmuting of oil into food, have enabled an expansion in plunder with no known precedent. And this revolution has freed the Dreamers to plunder not just the bodies of humans but the body of the Earth itself. The Earth is not our creation. It has no respect for us. It has no use for us. And its vengeance is not the fire in the cities but the fire in the sky.

Something more fierce than Marcus Garvey is riding on the whirlwind. Something more awful than all our African ancestors is rising with the seas. The two phenomena are known to each other. It was the cotton that passed through our chained hands that inaugurated this age. It is the flight from us that sent them sprawling into the subdivided woods. And the methods of transport through these new subdivisions, across the sprawl, is the automobile, the noose around the neck of the earth, and ultimately, the Dreamers themselves.

I drove away from the house of Mable Jones thinking of all of this. I drove away, as always, thinking of you. I do not believe that we can stop them, Samori, because they must ultimately stop themselves. And still I urge you to struggle. Struggle for the memory of your ancestors. Struggle for wisdom. Struggle for the warmth of The Mecca. Struggle for your grandmother and grandfather, for your name. But do not struggle for the Dreamers. Hope for them. Pray for them, if you are so moved. But do not pin your struggle on their conversion. The Dreamers will have to learn to struggle themselves, to understand that the field for their Dream, the stage where they have painted themselves white, is the deathbed of us all. The Dream is the same habit that endangers the planet, the same habit that sees our bodies stowed away in prisons and ghettos. I saw these ghettos driving back from Dr. Jones's home. They were the same ghettos I had seen in Chicago all those years ago, the same ghettos where my mother was raised, where my father was raised. Through the windshield I saw the mark of these ghettos—the abundance of beauty shops, churches, liquor stores, and crumbling housing—and I felt the old fear. Through the windshield I saw the rain coming down in sheets.

## ABOUT THE AUTHOR

TA-NEHISI COATES is a national correspondent for *The Atlantic* and the author of the memoir *The Beautiful Struggle.* Coates has received the National Magazine Award, the Hillman Prize for Opinion and Analysis Journalism, and the George Polk Award for his *Atlantic* cover story "The Case for Reparations." He lives in New York with his wife and son.

ABOUT THE TYPE

This book was set in Bembo, a typeface based on an old-style Roman face that was used for Cardinal Pietro Bembo's tract *De Aetna* in 1495. Bembo was cut by Francesco Griffo (1450–1518) in the early sixteenth century for Italian Renaissance printer and publisher Aldus Manutius (1449–1515). The Lanston Monotype Company of Philadelphia brought the well-proportioned letterforms of Bembo to the United States in the 1930s.